T0073937

Deep Learning Models for Medical Imaging

Deep Learning Models for Medical Imaging

KC Santosh

KC's PAMI Research Lab
Department of Computer Science
University of South Dakota
Vermillion, SD, United States

Nibaran Das

Computer Science and Engineering
Jadavpur University
Kolkata, India

Swarnendu Ghosh

Computer Science and Engineering
Jadavpur University
Kolkata, India

ACADEMIC PRESS

An imprint of Elsevier

Academic Press is an imprint of Elsevier
125 London Wall, London EC2Y 5AS, United Kingdom
525 B Street, Suite 1650, San Diego, CA 92101, United States
50 Hampshire Street, 5th Floor, Cambridge, MA 02139, United States
The Boulevard, Langford Lane, Kidlington, Oxford OX5 1GB, United Kingdom

Notices

Knowledge and best practice in this field are constantly changing. As new research and experience broaden our understanding, changes in research methods, professional practices, or medical treatment may become necessary.

Practitioners and researchers must always rely on their own experience and knowledge in evaluating and using any information, methods, compounds, or experiments described herein. In using such information or methods they should be mindful of their own safety and the safety of others, including parties for whom they have a professional responsibility.

To the fullest extent of the law, neither the Publisher nor the authors, contributors, or editors, assume any liability for any injury and/or damage to persons or property as a matter of products liability, negligence or otherwise, or from any use or operation of any methods, products, instructions, or ideas contained in the material herein.

Library of Congress Cataloging-in-Publication Data
A catalog record for this book is available from the Library of Congress

British Library Cataloguing-in-Publication Data
A catalogue record for this book is available from the British Library

ISBN: 978-0-12-823504-1

For information on all Academic Press publications
visit our website at https://www.elsevier.com/books-and-journals

Publisher: Mara Conner
Acquisitions Editor: Tim Pitts
Editorial Project Manager: Mariana L. Kuhl
Production Project Manager: Sojan P. Pazhayattil
Designer: Christian J. Bilbow

Typeset by VTeX

Contents

List of figures

List of tables

Authors

KC Santosh

Prof. KC Santosh is the Chair of the Department of Computer Science at the University of South Dakota (USD). Before joining USD, Prof. Santosh worked as a research fellow at the U.S. National Library of Medicine (NLM), National Institutes of Health (NIH). He was a postdoctoral research scientist at the LORIA research centre (with industrial partner, ITE-SOFT (France)). He has demonstrated expertise in artificial intelligence, machine learning, pattern recognition, computer vision, image processing and data mining with applications, such as medical imaging informatics, document imaging, biometrics, forensics, and speech analysis. His research projects are funded by multiple agencies, such as SDCRGP, Department of Education, National Science Foundation, and Asian Office of Aerospace Research and Development. He is the proud recipient of the Cutler Award for Teaching and Research Excellence (USD, 2021), the President's Research Excellence Award (USD, 2019), and the Ignite Award from the U.S. Department of Health and Human Services (2014). For more information, follow: http://kc-santosh.org and https://www.linkedin.com/company/kc-pami/ (research lab).

Nibaran Das

Nibaran Das received his B.Tech degree in Computer Science and Technology from Kalyani Govt. Engineering College under Kalyani University in 2003. He received his M.C.S.E. degree from Jadavpur University in 2005. He received his Ph.D. (Engg.) degree thereafter from Jadavpur University in 2012. He joined J.U. as a lecturer in 2006. His areas of current research interest are OCR of handwritten text, optimization techniques, image processing, and deep learning. He has been an editor of Bengali monthly magazine Computer Jagat since 2005.

Swarnendu Ghosh

Swarnendu Ghosh is an Assistant Professor at Adamas University in the Department of Computer Science and Engineering. He received his B.Tech degree in Computer Science and Engineering from West Bengal University of Technology in 2012. He received his Masters in Computer Science and Engineering from Jadavpur University in 2014. He has been a doctoral fellow under the Erasmus Mundus Mobility with Asia at University of Evora, Portugal. Currently he is continuing his Ph.D. in Computer Science and Engineering at Jadavpur University. His area of interest is deep learning, graph-based learning, and knowledge representation.

Foreword

I am pleased to write a foreword for "Deep Learning Models for Medical Imaging" by KC Santosh, Nibaran Das, and Swarnendu Ghosh. The authors are accomplished researchers in the field with expertise in medical image analysis and machine learning. This work is a comprehensive collection of chapters stemming from their prior work in the area.

Machine learning and medical image analysis has made significant advances in computational health research. In particular, recent advances in deep learning have made significant positive impact in the fields of biomedical research, data science, and computer aided diagnostics. The authors capture this energy in the field with a timely treatise on various efforts toward documenting advances. The book is organized into five chapters beginning with Chapter 1 providing a foundational introduction to machine learning and focusing on the basics of deep learning and its role in medical imaging. In Chapter 2, they delve further into providing a review of deep learning algorithms beginning with the basics of an artificial neural networks followed by convolutional neural networks and the encoded–decoder architecture. With these two chapters, even a naïve reader in the field should have a basic understanding of the content in the following chapters. Next, in Chapter 3 the book delves into various deep learning models that are commonly found in the literature. It should be noted that deep learning is a rapidly evolving field and new models and techniques are constantly being developed and published. However, even with such an active field, the authors have admirably described fundamental techniques upon with the reader can build a launch pad to delve deeper and grow their knowledge. Further, machine learning is a data-driven science. As such, it is critical for a researcher to obtain an understanding of the data they are working with, necessary preprocessing steps, and how they affect deep learning model selection and training. This chapter also describes common topics where deep learning is applied in medical imaging, viz., localization, segmentation, and classification. At this juncture, the reader is then led to two diverse types of medical images and, consequently, their deep learning-based analysis. In Chapter 4 the realm of microscopy images is explored through an example of cervical cytology. Microscopy images are typically imaged using whole-slide imagers, which result in extremely large files that are organized to allow specialized image viewers to show various magnifications. For deep learning algorithms to process such large images, the choice is to localize and segment objects (or regions) of interest before classifying them or analyze them at lowest magnification in their gestalt. The book discusses both kinds of images and uses the parlance of single-cell images and whole-slide images. The contents stimulate the reader into getting a good grasp on the challenges in the field and successes to date. In Chapter 5 the authors pick a current topic with COVID-19 pandemic image analysis. The chapter takes a broad view of the detecting, diagnosing, and predicting the disease outbreak and how deep learning-based networks have made an impact. The images that are discussed are contrary to microscopy images discussed prior. They discuss analysis of chest X-ray and chest CT (computed tomography) images.

In summary, the book is a meaningful contribution to the field and will provide the reader a solid background in the field of deep learning-based medical image analysis. The journey, like the method, is deep and intellectually stimulating. The book provides a sound launch pad for the reader.

Sameer Antani

National Library of Medicine,
National Institutes of Health, Bethesda, MD, United States

Preface

Medical imaging is no exception when we consider technological advances of deep learning algorithms in computer vision. Considering diverse data, the objective of the book is to advocate "no to feature engineering" since hand-crafted features require prior domain knowledge. However, even though we have a rich set of state-of-the-art algorithms, no generic deep learning model can be applied when expert-based decisions are required, such as medical imaging tools.

The book aims to provide a thorough concept of deep learning, its importance in medical imaging and/or healthcare with two different case studies: a) cytology image analysis and b) coronavirus (COVID-19) prediction, screening, and decision-making. Both of them use publicly available datasets in their experiments. Of many deep learning models, custom convolutional neural network (CNN), ResNet, InceptionNet, and DenseNet are considered in our experiments. Our results follow "with" and "without" transfer learning (including different optimization solutions), in addition to the use of data augmentation and ensemble networks.

The book covers a wide range of readers starting from early career research scholars and professors/scientists to industrialists.

Acronyms

AI	Artificial Intelligence
A2I	Artificial and Augmented Intelligence
AUC	Area Under the Curve
ADALINE	Adaptive Linear Unit
CNN	Convolutional Neural Network
CAC	Coronary Artery Calcium
CUDA	Compute Unified Device Architecture
CT	Computed Tomography
CXR	Chest X-ray
CSF	Cerebrospinal Fluid
DL	Deep Learning
DNN	Deep Neural Network
FCN	Fully Connected Network
FNA	Fine Needle Aspiration
GIA	Gastrointestinal Angiectasia
GPU	Graphics Processing Unit
LSTM	Long Short-Term Memory
MRI	Magnetic Resonance Imaging
MRC	Medical Research Council
ML	Machine Learning
NN	Neural Network
PET	Positron Emission Tomography
ReLu	Rectified Linear Unit
RNN	Recurrent Neural Network
R-CNN	Regio-based CNN
SIR	Susceptible-Infectious-Recovered
SBCE	Small Bowel Capsule Endoscopy
WHO	World Health Organization
WCE	Wireless Capsule Endoscopy
YOLO	You Only Look Once

CHAPTER 1

Introduction

1.1 Background

Technological advancements have always played an important role in data analysis, visualization, and decision-making. Of all, artificial intelligence (AI) has been driving merely all kinds of data originated from several different sources, where signal processing and pattern recognition, computer vision, data mining, and machine learning play crucial role.

The seeds of artificial intelligence can be traced back to the works of Sir Alan Turing during the 2nd world war when he cracked the German code for communication by applying heuristics to shrink the solution space [1]. In the following years, several factors such as the works of Donald Hebb [2], the 1956 Dartmouth conference and funding agencies, such as DARPA, spurred the onset of AI. In the successive decades, there were several ups and downs or rise and fall of several technologies. However, in the last two decades, the growth of AI has accelerated due to several reasons, such as development of hardware with increased computational capabilities, availability of large quantities of high-quality datasets, and the introduction of an array of extremely efficient statistical machine learning techniques under the commonly used term of deep learning. The primary reason behind this is avoiding feature engineering that could vary from one data type to another.

Broadly, AI-driven tools and techniques click a variety of sectors, such as education [3], communication [4], transportation [5], agriculture [6], entertainment, finance [7], and healthcare [8–10]. Considering the size of the world and sensitiveness of the data, healthcare has been considered the important and unavoidable domain to be taken care of.

Among the various deep learning algorithms, the introduction of convolutional neural networks (CNN) [11] had significant impact on the field of computer vision. Not to be confused, the aforementioned reasons were also highly appreciated. CNNs are found to be useful in many of the previously mentioned domains. Importantly, some of the most important contributions of deep learning algorithms have been seen in the field of healthcare, or more specifically in the domain of medical imaging [12,13]. Imaging techniques play an extremely important role in the field of healthcare as common medical procedures start with screening [14–17] and diagnosis [18] to decision-making. Imaging techniques are also necessary for other tasks, such as automatically locating regions of interest [19], rotation detection [20], and even image view classification (e.g., chest X-rays [21]). An image speaks thousands of words. The images come with a variety of challenges depending on sources of the images. Medical imaging practices can be carried out using a variety of imaging devices that can incorporate different types of sensors, magnification levels, spectrums, and so on. Thus a vast area of modern challenges (e.g., COVID-19 screening [22–24]) can be addressed by building smart systems for medical imaging analysis. Few noticeable and recent works on COVID-19 screening, decision-making and impact can be found at [9,17,25–27].

Overall, the book is aimed to provide a clear idea on a) the rise of AI-driven tools/techniques in medical imaging and b) technology acceleration due to deep learning models/architectures. With such notes, the objective of the book is providing an understanding of deep learning models that are commonly used to handle a variety of medical images.

The chapter is organized as follows. Section 1.2 provides a machine learning fundamentals and its types. It includes supervised, unsupervised, semisupervised, reinforcement learning algorithms. Section 1.3 provides how machine learning algorithms have been used for a variety of problems, where three learning mechanisms are discussed: rule-based learning, feature-based learning, and representational learning. In Section 1.4, we discuss deep learning basics. Importance and its popularity are discussed in Section 1.5. Section 1.6 discusses recent works in deep learning for medical images. The scope of the book is neatly discussed in Section 1.7.

1.2 Machine learning and its types

Before proceeding to deep learning, let us have a quick and broad overview of machine learning. In simple terms, machine learning algorithms refer to computational techniques that can find a way to connect a set of inputs to a desired set of outputs by learning relevant data. As defined by Tom Mitchell [28],

> "A program is said to **learn** from experience E with respect to some class of tasks T and performance measure P, if its performance at tasks in T, as measured by P, improves with experience E."

This means that a machine learning algorithm attempts to approximate a function f by analyzing the input data distribution that would produce a desired output satisfying some predefined requirements. It is also expected for the machine learning algorithm to reduce the uncertainty in the approximation as it is exposed to more data samples.

Machine learning techniques can be classified into four major categories based on data type(s) and objective(s).

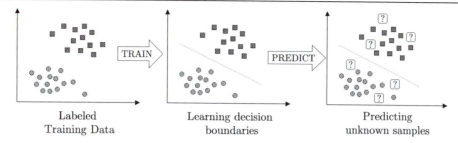

Figure 1.1: An example of supervised learning showing training using labeled samples (red squares and blue circles) and predicting the class of unseen samples (question marks).

1) *Supervised learning:*

Human beings learn from various places. One of the obvious ways to learn efficiently is through proper supervision that helps them to make sense of their environment and guides them with appropriate actions. In machine learning, supervision is particularly useful when data samples are labeled. If a the desired output for a sample **x** is **y**, then a supervised learning algorithm attempts to approximate a function f that produces a similar output $\hat{\mathbf{y}}$,

$$\hat{\mathbf{y}} = f(\mathbf{x}). \tag{1.1}$$

The algorithm is said to learn if the difference between **y** and $\hat{\mathbf{y}}$ progressively reduces as the algorithm is exposed to more samples. A performance metric such as accuracy or error can be used to compute this difference and to evaluate whether the performance of the learning algorithm is within acceptable thresholds. A demonstration can be seen in Fig. 1.1.

Supervised algorithms can come in two flavors, namely, discriminative and generative techniques. Discriminative learning or classification aims to categorize input samples to one or several of a predefined set of classes. The mapping function $f : \mathbb{R}^n \rightarrow \{1, \ldots, k\}$ maps an n-dimensional input to one or several of the k classes. The output can also be represented as a k-dimensional probability distribution or even k binomial distributions for problems with multiple positive classes. Generative machine learning aims to generate real-valued outputs to signify a specific concept. Here the mapping function is defined as $f : \mathbb{R}^n \rightarrow \mathbb{R}$.

From a probabilistic perspective, supervised learning is aptly represented by the Bayes theorem:

$$P(Y|X) = \frac{P(X|Y) \cdot P(Y)}{P(X)}. \tag{1.2}$$

The equation attempts to compute a posterior distribution $P(Y|X)$, which predicts the probability of a class for a sample. This is computed by multiplying the prior distribution

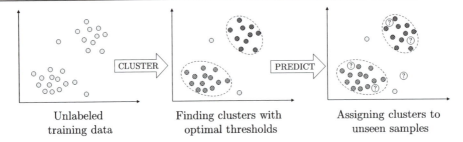

Figure 1.2: An example of unsupervised learning showing clustering unlabeled samples (circles) into two clusters and predicting the clusters corresponding to unseen samples (question marks).

of the classes $P(Y)$, which corresponds to the skewness of the class distribution, and the estimated likelihood $P(X|Y)$ of a sample for a given class. This is signifies the underlying mapping function that associates classes with corresponding features. The learning algorithm simply maximizes the likelihood estimate. The denominator $P(X)$ is known as evidence and is generally a measure of how well the hyperplane separates the different classes. A higher number of samples on a specific side of a hyperplane increases the uncertainty of prediction and hence inversely affects the posterior probability.

2) *Unsupervised learning:*

Though supervision can quickly help in learning specific concepts, it is not always possible to obtain supervision for all kinds of tasks. Human beings depend on their ability to analyze their environment to find out recurrent patterns and still make some sense of completely unknown objects. Kids are often seen possessing a high amount of curiosity where they try to interact with every new objects that they see and often associate them with similar objects that they have encountered in the past. This phenomenon can also be implemented by adopting unsupervised learning techniques as shown in Fig. 1.2. In real world, data acquisition often tends to be a much easier task than data annotation. In that case, unsupervised algorithms can be used to make sense of the data distribution. This type of learning systems look for patterns in a dataset without predefined labels and with minimum human supervision. Whereas supervised algorithms try to infer a likelihood estimate $P(X|Y)$, unsupervised algorithms analyze the a priori data distribution $P(X)$. The pattern recognition methods revolve around in density estimation of samples in the input space and formation of clusters of similar observations. Other approaches also focus on estimation of multivariate and marginal distributions to obtain principal components. Principal components corresponding to the eigenvectors of the data distribution can be used for various feature extraction techniques, which is very useful for clustering algorithms. Other applications of unsupervised learning can be the use of generative models to synthesize realistic data samples, which have various application in fields such as augmented reality and so on.

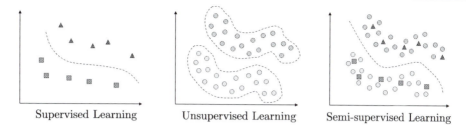

Figure 1.3: Semisupervised learning: Involves a mixture of unlabeled and labeled samples for efficient prediction.

3) *Semisupervised learning:*

Human beings are exposed to both forms of learning techniques, supervised and unsupervised. Human beings as they grow up, often learn to associate vast quantities of data with a little amount of supervised data that they have been taught. A child who is taught to recognize cats and dogs as animals and bikes and cars as vehicles will also learn to differentiate between other types of animals and vehicles. This innate ability of generalized learning comes from their capacity to associate their supervised concepts with the unsupervised patterns that they have observed.

Although unsupervised algorithms can be very useful to make sense of unlabeled data, they often fall below the acceptable threshold. Many factors such as variance in the sample space and noise introduce a fuzziness in the clustering process. On the other hand, supervised techniques can boast much more accurate separation; however, the certainty is governed by the number of annotated samples. With low number of samples, there is a higher chance of uncertainty in prediction. With further increase in the degree of freedom the approximation function overfits the training data and fails to perform for unseen samples. Semisupervised algorithms can provide good results in these cases. On one hand, with a little bit of annotated data, clustering algorithms can reduce the fuzziness by a great extent. A demonstration can be found in Fig. 1.3. One-shot learning techniques implement ideas like these to classify large quantity of unlabeled data with supervision on a subset. Similarly, using density estimation of a large amount of unlabeled data, supervised classification algorithms can produce a better fit for the labeled samples that are more regularized as compared to before. Transfer learning algorithms often use the concepts from unsupervised techniques on large data samples to enhance performance on smaller-sized supervised algorithms to predict a better fit for the input distribution.

4) *Reinforcement learning:*

Human beings often achieve success in a problem by stacking multiple decisions while interacting with the environment. At the end of the series of decisions or actions, their success or failure enriches their experience, which allows them take better decisions in the future. This can be easily seen in things like board games where the success in the game

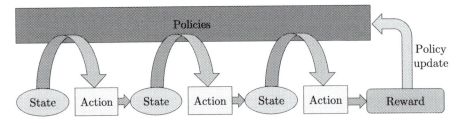

Figure 1.4: Reinforcement learning: a sequence of states determined by actions defined by policies yielding a reward at the end. The reward can be used to update policies.

depends on series of actions that maximizes their chances of success as they progress. At any point of time the decisions are mostly reactions to the current state of environment and are based on the experience that they have gathered from previous games. Reinforcement learning algorithms [29] model simulations like these where the machine learns to respond to an environmental state with appropriate actions with a goal to maximize a reward. The method of selecting the action is called a policy (π). A state value function $V_\pi(s)$ tracks the expected reward if a specific state s is followed by a sequence of actions defined by a policy π. The goal of reinforcement learning is finding out an action-value function that optimally associates and action with an environmental state so that the reward is maximized. A graphical demonstration is shown in Fig. 1.4.

1.3 Evolution of machine learning

Since their introduction, machine learning technologies have always driven by the complexity of data and learning objective(s). The evolution of machine learning can roughly be seen as a method of cascading modules of automation. In each phase of the evolution, various modes of human involvement in the process of learning are automated (Fig. 1.5). By carefully analyzing this trend it is quite possible to predict the direction in which learning technologies are progressing. Broadly, let us discuss on a) rule-based, b) feature-based, and c) representation learning.

1.3.1 Rule-based learning

Early days, AI community was governed by rule-based systems [30]. By manually analyzing the data a set of handcrafted rules were composed to carry out intelligent tasks. As an example, a tic-tac-toe game can be considered, which can be easily defined/explained by a set of rules, such as:

•   If there exists a threat, then mark the third empty slot; otherwise.

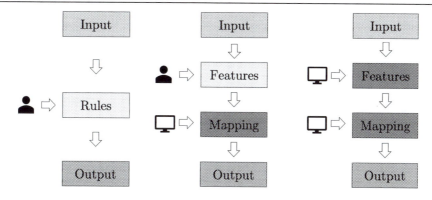

Rule based system   Feature based learning   Representation learning

Figure 1.5: Evolution of machine learning: yellow (light gray in print version) determines user-defined operations and green (dark gray in print version) defines automated operations carried out by intelligent agent.

- If a fork is possible, then mark appropriately; otherwise.
- Capture center square if free; otherwise.
- If opponent has captured a corner, then mark the opposite corner; otherwise.
- Capture any empty square.

Rule-based systems are viable for small-scale problems. For large-scale problems, there were two main issues. Firstly, the objective itself can be too complex to hand-craft appropriate rules. Secondly, real-world data samples are often represented in a high-dimensional space. The curse of dimensionality states that the number of dimensions has an exponential impact on the size of the search space. This makes pattern recognition an extremely difficult task. This gave rise to the feature-based learning techniques.

1.3.2 Feature-based learning

Although hand-crafted rules are functional, they are extremely tedious and sometimes infeasible for humans. Human cognitive abilities are often judged by their ability to respond to stimuli and carry out actions. For a machine, it can be represented as a generating some desired output values based on some input values. An intelligent method for solving a cognitive problem can be roughly defined as approximating a function f that maps the input space $\mathbf{x}$ to the output space $\mathbf{y}$. Any machine learning technique in its most generic form would attempt to formulate this function:

$$\mathbf{y} = f(\mathbf{x}). \tag{1.3}$$

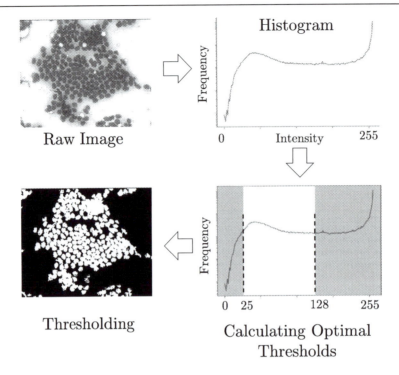

Figure 1.6: An example of feature-based learning showing histogram-based thresholding.

If **x** has a high dimensionality of representation, then the function becomes harder to approximate. Feature-based techniques [31] thrive on the ability to extract compressed nonredundant information from data samples. Features of sample are defined as some concise descriptors of the raw samples that can express their exclusive properties. A nice example of feature extraction can be seen in case of histogram-based thresholding. This is a method to binarize a grayscale image by automatically calculating an optimal threshold point. A 256×256 image with 8-bit pixels (256 different levels) can be represented by a 2^{16}-dimensional vector consisting of numbers between 0 and 255. As shown in Fig. 1.6, instead of computing the statistical distribution directly on the image, a histogram can be used, which serves as a feature. A histogram consists of the frequency of the 256 different levels across the image. The representation of the image is reduced from 2^{16} to 2^8 dimensions but still has enough information to compute a threshold level such that the interclass variance is maximum. Moreover, this process can convert images of any size to a fixed dimension that aptly describes the intensity distribution. Feature-based learning techniques have been often used to handle various complicated tasks. Various machine learnings see a significant boost in speed and performance when they operate on carefully designed features instead of the raw data.

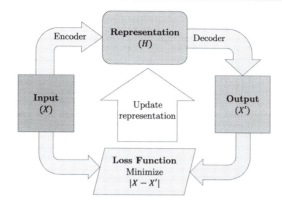

Figure 1.7: Automatic representation learning uses an encoder and decoder to reconstruct the input while learning a compressed representation in the process.

1.3.3 Representation learning

Although feature-based learning is quite efficient to perform in various scenarios, it has some major drawbacks. Handcrafting features require domain experts, which may not be always available for all kinds of problems. Moreover, the workflow necessary for designing good features is not generic or reusable for other domains. They are highly specific toward the dataset and are an obvious hindrance in terms of reusability. Another issue is the lack of scalability. As the task gets more complicated with higher dimensionality, more intraclass variance, and higher number of categories, it gets harder to design appropriate features. The obvious next step is the automation of feature extraction techniques. Representation learning [32] aims to work with raw input samples and find out generic ways to extract features. In the field of neural network-based machine learning, the early attempts of representation learning were seen in the implementation of autoassociative neural networks [33,34] or more commonly known as autoencoders. As demonstrated in Fig. 1.7, autoencoders comprise of an encoder and a decoder. Each of these modules are composed of stacked layers of neurons that transform the input data. The encoder creates a compressed representation of the input space, and decoder attempts to recreate the input space from the compressed dimensions. As the objective function minimizes the difference between the reconstruction from the decoder and the actual input, the compressed representation effectively provides us with a low-dimensional equivalent of the input sample to work with. The growth of neural network-based systems flourished since the introduction of back-propagation algorithm [35], which can tune parameters across the multiple layers of nonlinear regression units called neurons. The depth of these layers generally affects the order of the approximation function. Whereas shallower layers encode low-level features, deeper layers encoder high-level features. With the increase in the complexity of problems and datasets, deeper networks became a necessity. Thus deep learning [36,37] was born to cope with the challenges of implementing multilayered neural networks with greater depth for modeling complex concepts by creating a hierarchical structure of feature extraction modules. As mentioned before, these layers begin with low-level features and combine them to create high-level features in deeper layers.

1.4 Basics to deep learning

Deep learning may have caused a revolution in the field of machine learning over the last few decades. This is a consequence of more than 70 years of neural network (NN) based research and development in computer science and engineering. The earliest seeds can be traced back to the studies by Donald Hebb regarding the cognitive capabilities of human beings [2]. The evolution of the NNs can broadly be classified into three eras as follows.

1.4.1 The rise of cybernetics

The earliest attempts to model human cognition were made by Donald Hebb [2]. In his work, he proposed a neuroscientific theory, which claimed that synaptic efficacy rises due to repeated and persistent stimulation of post synaptic cell. It is one of the earliest models that introduces how neurons in our brains learn in a computationally understandable terms. This is one of the key works that spurred the domain of neural networks. A comparison of biological neural networks and artificial neural networks is shown in Fig. 1.8.

The first artificial neuron was proposed in [38], where a neuron was defined as a single decision-making unit that can accept multiple signals and can decide to activate if necessary. The activation of a neuron generates an output signal. This basic model of artificial neuron was further improved in [39] (shown in Fig. 1.9), where the proposed perceptron model was able to train a set of weights by observing the data using adaptive linear units or ADALINE [40], thus providing us with the first learnable neural model. The idea behind the artificial neuron will be discussed thoroughly in Section 2.2.1.

The excitement that started to rise due to works like these inspired the Dartmouth conference [41], which recognized AI as a legitimate domain of research and began what is now one of the most booming sectors of modern technology. Let us repeat that the term AI was first coined in the Dartmouth workshop organized by John McCarthy in 1956. The proposal for the workshop stated the following:

"We propose that a 2-month, 10-man study of artificial intelligence be carried out during the summer of 1956 at Dartmouth College in Hanover, New Hampshire. The study is to proceed on the basis of the conjecture that every aspect of learning or any other feature of intelligence

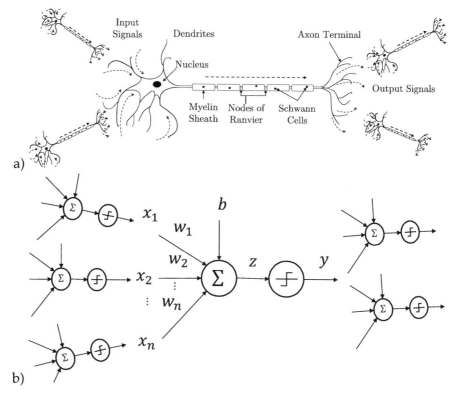

Figure 1.8: A graphical comparison between a) a biological neural network and b) an artificial neuron.

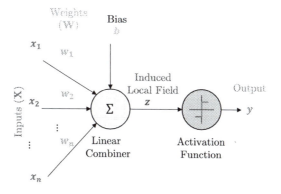

Figure 1.9: Perceptron: a unit of artificial neural networks.

can in principle be so precisely described that a machine can be made to simulate it. An attempt will be made to find how to make machines use language, form abstractions and concepts, solve kinds of problems now reserved for humans, and improve themselves. We

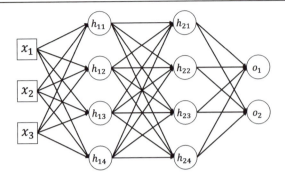

Figure 1.10: A multilayered perceptron showing neurons arranged in different layers.

think that a significant advance can be made in one or more of these problems if a carefully selected group of scientists work on it together for a summer."

The era of cybernetics thrived for sometime before a major flaw of the perceptron model was observed [42]. Perceptrons were generally composed of neurons that can be trained to model a linear regression problem. This made them unable to model nonlinear functions like XOR. Although stacking up multiple neurons can solve the problems like these with multiple straight hyperplanes, there was no generalized training protocol to support networks like those.

1.4.2 The connectionist movement

Several other works started to rise up during this era that implemented for feature learning Boltzmann machines [43]. The idea was to represent input by multiple set of neurons and stack up layers of such neurons to approximate complex functions as shown in Fig. 1.10. With backpropagation, it was much easier to iteratively train networks.

During this era, the ideas of representation learning were also beginning to be explored. Autoencoders were trained to create compressed meaningful representation of data without any supervision [34]. Similarly, self-organizing feature maps were also proposed to perform feature extraction in an unsupervised environment [44]. A study was made on the striate cortex of a cat to understand the structure of visual receptors [45]. It was observed that the visual cortex is made up of a various layers of localized receptors. This idea later inspired the development of CNNs [11]. Moreover, neural networks were also beginning to emerge as a sequential learning model such as Hopfield networks [46] and recurrent neural networks (RNNs) [35,47]. As the topology of networks became wider and deeper, new problems started to emerge. Though it was presumed that depth was necessary to handle more complicated

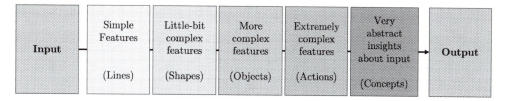

Building upon simpler features to learn more complex features

Figure 1.11: The fundamental concept of deep learning.

tasks, it came with several problems like vanishing or exploding gradients and computational overhead.

1.4.3 The onset of deep learning

The fundamental concept of deep learning is representing complex features using multiple stacked layers of feature extracting neurons. The depth of the network is necessary to build complex features by combining simpler features from shallower layers. This concept is graphically demonstrated in Fig. 1.11. The back-propagation rewrites the global error gradient as a chain of partial derivatives of each operation in the computational tree. As the depth of the network increases, the length of the chain also increases. Due to multiplication of too many gradients, the values often tend toward zero or infinity. This created a vanishing or exploding gradient problem which significantly affected the weight updating protocol [48]. Either updating would stop due to very small gradients weight or make major leaps due to too high gradients. Either way convergence was affected. This was especially significant for sequential learning models like RNN that failed to capture long-term dependencies.

One of the earliest models addressing this issue and successfully implementing deep neural networks without loss of gradients was the long short-term memory (LSTM) network for sequential learning [49]. Moreover, various feature extraction and image processing techniques involved convolution of filters. Building on this idea and upon further inspiration of the work by Hubel and Wiesel [45], which demonstrated the localized receptors of visual cortex in animals, convolutional neural networks were proposed [11]. Though convolutional neural networks or CNNs came with huge computational overhead, the results were astounding, and the method itself was an extremely generalized model, which can automatically extract a set of appropriate features from a set of labeled images. With the involvement of GPU-based computing spurred by the CUDA [50] library, the computation overhead was addressed, which set the platform for the growth of deep learning techniques [51].

1.4.4 Motivation: deep learning

The massive increase in deep learning-based applications has two main driving forces. One of them is an increased amount of computational resources. Graphics processing units (GPUs) were primarily built to handle complex graphics-oriented tasks in distributed environment. Deep learning networks like CNNs and LSTM networks can also use this distributed environment as most of the operations involved are basic linear algebra. The release of the CUDA API[1] by Nvidia allowed researchers to parallelize trains and evaluate their deep neural networks to avoid possible computational complexity.

Another factor behind the success of deep learning is the availability of large amount of curated data [52,53]. With rising speed of internet connectivity, large amount of data is becoming available. With services like Amazon Mechanical Turk, many large datasets have been organized, cleaned, and annotated for training deep learning models. These models not only perform well on the respective datasets, but also they can be used as pretrained models for transfer learning applications [54]. Further, several international challenges attract researchers across the globe to provide models for tasks in different domains.

1.5 Importance of deep learning

The introduction of deep learning techniques caused a revolution in the field of computer vision and machine learning. The era of deep learning is defined by three main factors.

1) The first is the ability to learn from raw data without the necessity of handcrafted features. Raw samples like original images often contain lots of redundant information, noise, and large variance. Early works like auto-encoder and recurrent neural networks attempted to extract features from raw samples but lacked the necessary depth and redundancy resolution to process complex spatial features or sequential data of long lengths. The introduction of CNNs allowed us to learn complex spatial features by stacking up locally sensitive kernels that were convoluted across the entire image, whereas long short-term memory networks provided a way to extract time sensitive features from sequential data with the loss of gradients over large depths.

2) The second major factor is the depth of the network. It was already known that deeper networks are better for representation of complex functions. However, gradient propagation across depth is a hindrance as gradients tend to vanish or explode due to multiple multiplications in the chain of partial derivatives. The early struggles in the field of deep learning mainly focused on methods preserving gradients to enable back-propagation in deeper networks. Though long short-term memory networks tackled the issue of depth

---

[1] https://developer.nvidia.com/cuda-zone.

for sequential learning models, the domain of computer vision was still constricted in that regard. CNNs were effective enough to extract features from image datasets with high variance. However, after a certain number of layers, gradient propagations stopped due to vanishing gradients. The first major breakthrough was achieved by restricted Boltzmann machines that implement layerwise training to preserve gradients. This resulted in the formulation of the deep belief networks. Subsequently, the introduction of rectified linear units for activation addressed the issue of vanishing gradients and led to the formation of the AlexNet [55] which was capable to provide extremely good performance on the 1000-class classification problem stated by the ILSVRC [56].

3) The above to features of deep learning techniques make it a potent tool for a large number of problems. Therefore the third factor behind the success of deep learning techniques is the broad spectrum of problems addressed by them. Following are some of the most important learning tasks that can be addressed by deep learning techniques:

– Classification:

Classification tasks involve the categorization of samples into a set of predefined classes. A large number of CNNs [11,55,57–59] are built for performing image classification.

– Detection and Localization:

Detection and localization are further refinement of the classification task, where the presence of multiple objects must be detected in the scene along with their location [60,61]. Many works like R-CNN [62–64] and YOLO [65–67] can perform simultaneous detection and localization.

– Segmentation:

Localization provides an output in the form of an approximate location of an object in a scene, often in the form of a bounding box. For a finer level detection, we can go for segmentation [68] that performs a pixel level classification to pinpoint exact posture of the object in the image. This is particularly suitable for deformable objects and has lots of application scenarios such as surveillance, autonomous driving, medical imaging, and so on. Segmentation algorithms often rely on encoder–decoder architectures [69–71] to generate a pixel-level probability distribution of the same size as that of the image.

– Conceptualization:

So far we have talked about recognition, detection, and segmentation of image. But overall concept understanding of an image is one of the toughest tasks. Understanding concepts is a key for various applications like caption generation [72], visual question answering [73], relation extraction [74], action detection [75], and so on.

– Sequential Learning:

Deep learning techniques are also applicable for sequential learning problems such as video processing or natural language processing. Some of the most promising advances in this field can be seen in works like LSTM [49] or gated recurrent modules [76]. Other applications of sequential learning include tasks such as instance detection, time-series analysis, and graph-based analysis.

—   Embedding:
Embedding is another key application area of deep learning. Embedding refers to the representation of raw data samples as tensors such that similar samples will be close together in the embedding space [77]. Embedding has vast applications in areas such as content-based retrieval [78], text processing [79], and semantic analysis.

1.6 Deep learning in medical imaging: a review

The healthcare industry heavily depend on visual representations of different parts of the body. There are several methods of capturing images that vary in terms of nature of camera, type of spectrum scanned, and the scale in which the image is captured. Different types of medical imaging techniques can convey different types of information about different body parts.

Before we delve into reviewing deep learning techniques on medical images, let us understand the different types of medical imaging techniques.

1.6.1 Medical imaging scope

Medical imaging techniques have been a key part of clinical procedures. There are several ways to create visual representations of our human body to allow medical practitioners to diagnose and treat different kinds of diseases. We discuss some of the commonly used imaging techniques.

1) *Radiography:*
Radiography is an imaging technique using X-rays, gamma rays, or similar radiation to view the internal form of an object (see Fig. 1.12). Images can be produced either as two-dimensional photographic films, or in case of computed tomography, a three-dimensional representation is generated by combining multidimensional x-rays across various cross sectional planes. Radiography is used to detect the presence or absence of a disease, structural damages or anomalies or locate foreign objects.

2) *Magnetic resonance imaging:*
Unlike radiography, MRI uses strong magnetic field gradients and radio waves to generate images of various organs in the body (see Fig. 1.13). MRIs produce much sharper images than CT scans and have many applications. MRIs are typically used to find anomalies in the brain and the spinal cord, locate tumors, cysts and other anomalies in the human body,

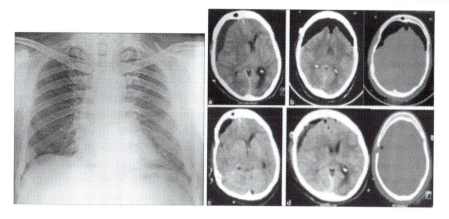

Figure 1.12: Radiographs: chest x-ray (left) and CT scan (right).

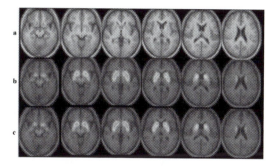

Figure 1.13: MRI images.

breast cancer screening, injuries or abnormalities in joints such as back and knee, detect certain types of heart problems, diseases in liver or other abdominal organs, fibroids, endometriosis, or analyze uterine anomalies, and so on.

3) *Ultrasonography:*

Ultrasonography refers to the visualization of various internal tissues by mapping how high-frequency sound waves are reflected by them (see Fig. 1.14). This is often used to monitor unborn babies and also to understand causes of pain and swelling in internal organs.

4) *Endoscopy:*

Unlike other methods, endoscopy is an intrusive procedure where a device is inserted inside hollow organs to capture images (see Fig. 1.15). Endoscopy finds its uses in those cases where hyperspectral imaging is not enough and real photograph of the internal organ is necessary. It has huge applications during surgeries. It can be used to examine numerous body parts such as respiratory tract, gastrointestinal tract, reproductive tract, urinary tract, or even closed body cavities.

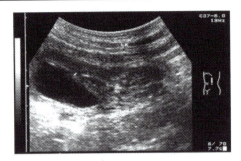

Figure 1.14: USG images.

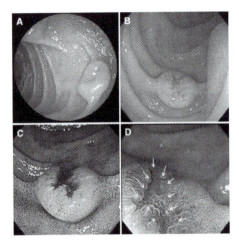

Figure 1.15: Endoscopy image sample.

5) *Positron emission tomography:*
   A nuclear medicine functional imaging technique is used to observe metabolic processes in the body as an aid to the diagnosis of disease. The imaging protocol is carried out by introducing a radioactive tracer in the system of the subject that can track various metabolic process in various organs. This type of scanning can sometimes detect diseases before it shows up on other imaging tests. A positron emission tomography (PET) scan is an effective way to analyze the chemical activities in various parts of the body (see Fig. 1.16). It can be used to identify several conditions including cancers, heart diseases, and brain disorders.

6) *Microscopic imaging:*
   Microscopic imaging is used in various cytological and histological diagnosis (see Fig. 1.17). They basically deal with images captured in the cellular or tissue level and can aid in various clinical treatments. This type of imaging can be used to analyze various

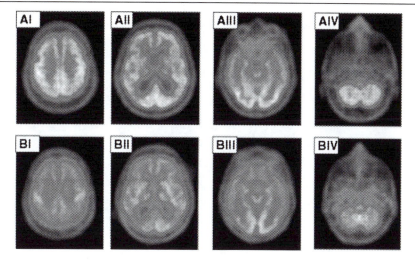

Figure 1.16: PET image.

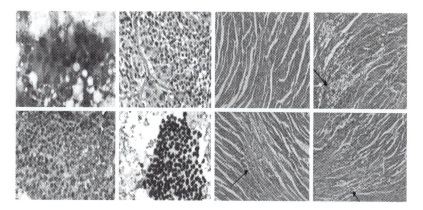

Figure 1.17: Microscopic images for cytology (left) and histology (right).

parts of the body at a cellular level to provide significant information about the different types of tissues and organs in the body. It can be used to diagnose or screen for cancer, fetal abnormalities, pap smears, infectious organisms, and several other screening or diagnostic areas.

7) *Ophthalmoscopy:*

Ophthalmoscopy, also called fundoscopy, is a test that allows a health professional to see inside the fundus of the eye (see Fig. 1.18). It is used to detect retinal detachment or eye diseases such as glaucoma. A swollen optic disc can indicate high intracranial pressure that can occur due to hydrocephalus, benign intracranial hypertension, or brain tumors. They are also necessary to screen diabetic retinopathy.

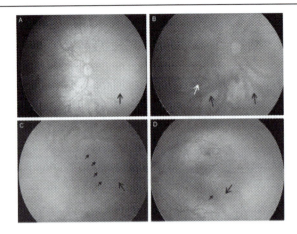

Figure 1.18: Ophthalmoscopic images.

Table 1.1:   Popular classification tasks for medical images.

Challenge	Association	Description
PALM	ISBI 2019	Pathologic myopia challenge
ACDC-LungHP	ISBI 2019	Automatic cancer detection and classification
EAD 2019	ISBI 2019	Endoscopic artefact detection
CheXpert	–	Abnormality detection in chest radiograph
PatchCamelyon	Kaggle	Metastatic cancer identification
BreastPathQ	SPIE Medical Imaging	Cancer cellularity scoring for tumor burden assessment
B-ALL	ISBI 2019	Leukemic cell recognition
PROSTATEx	Grand Challenges	Prostrate lesion classification using MRI Data
REFUGE	MICCAI 2018	Retinal fundus glaucoma detection
IDRiD	ISBI 2018	Detection and grading of diabetic retinopathy
MURA	–	Abnormality detection in musculoskeletal radiographs
ImageCLEF TB	CLEF 18	Tuberculosis categorization
Melanoma detection	MICCAI 2018	Diagnosis of melanoma from dermoscopic images
Pancreatic cancer	MICCAI 2018	Survival probability prediction from pancreatic CT scans
BraTS	MICCAI 2018	Survival prediction using preoperative MRI Scans
Pathology classification	MICCAI 2018	Glioma tumor classification

1.6.2 Medical imaging data

Previously, we have seen various types of medical imaging techniques that exist in today's world. With each of these domains, there exist unique sets of challenges, leading to a variety of related computer vision applications. Different types of intelligent systems can be built that can detect the presence of anomalies, localize regions of interests, segment various organs, or even classify the images into relevant categories. Some popular challenges are listed in Table 1.1.

1.6.3 Applications: deep learning in medical imaging

Most of the interpretation of medical images are done by medical experts, and for each type of imaging a very specific set of experts are needed with specific medical backgrounds. Until lately, traditional learning techniques heavily depended on features collected by medical experts. But with deep learning techniques the feature extraction technique can be highly automated greatly reducing the dependence on medical personnel and reducing diagnosis time. Deep learning techniques have been implemented in several medical imaging applications till date. We discuss some of them.

1) *Diabetic retinopathy:*

   According to World Health Organization, 422 million people suffered from diabetes in 2014, and diabetes is one of the major causes behind diabetic retinopathy that leads to blindness. However, when diagnosed at an early stage, it can be controlled and even cured. A CNN-based model [80] is used to classify between moderate and worse referable diabetic retinopathy. The work was done in collaboration with the Google AI Team. In [81] the authors also trained a CNN with dropouts on publicly available DRIVE, STARE, and Kaggle datasets for diabetic retinopathic image classification.

2) *Histological and microscopical element detection:*

   In [82] the authors showed a way to detect and classify colon cancer using spatially constrained CNNs in the CRCHistoPhenotypes Dataset.[2] In [83] the authors demonstrated the benefit of using transfer learning to cope up with low number of data samples. The authors demonstrated the use of CNNs to detect malaria, tuberculosis, and hookworm from pap smear datasets [84].

3) *Gastrointestinal disease detection:*

   Starting from the mouth to the anus, the gastrointestinal tract consists of several organs and can exhibit several common diseases. Ulcers cause bleeding in the upper gastrointestinal tract. Cancer, polyps, or diverticulitis can cause bleeding from the large intestine. Crohn, celiac, ulcers, tumors, and bleeding owing to abnormal blood vessels can occur in the small intestine.

   In [85,86] the authors used the CNN models to detect bleeding in organs using wireless capsule endoscopy (WCE). [87] used CNNs to detect gastrointestinal angiectasia (GIA) in small bowel capsule endoscopy (SBCE). The networks were designed to perform classification and semantic segmentation. Colonoscopy is also often done for colorectal cancer prevention. In [88] the authors used CNNs for to improve the adenoma detection rate.

---

2 warwick.ac.uk/fac/sci/dcs/research/tia/data/crchistolabelednucleihe/.

4) *Cardiac imaging:*

CT and MRI scans are often used for various cardiac imaging applications. Coronary artery calcium (CAC) scoring is a time-consuming task and a hindrance for epidemiological studies. In [89] the authors described several deep neural networks and discussed various areas that can be applied for cardiovascular disease. Applications include plaque risk assessment by classification, CAC scoring by regression, ejection fraction estimation by segmentation, content-based image retrieval by automatic report generation, and CT dose reduction by synthetic image generation.

5) *Tumor detection:*

Tumors refer to abnormal growth of cells in any part of the body to create a distinct mass of tissue. Medical imaging has huge impact in the area of tumor detection as it is one of the primary way of diagnosis. Given the chronic nature of tumors, if they become malignant, then it is essential to build advanced algorithms to swiftly detect their presence. In [90] the authors provided one of the initial research for detecting tumors in mammograms. This was very beneficial for automatic breast cancer detection. Authors also introduced a ResNet50 and VGG16-based network to detect benign calcification, malignant calcification, benign mass, and malignant mass [91].

6) *Alzheimer and Parkinson detection:*

Both Alzheimer and Parkinson are neurological disorders that progressively deteriorate over time and can lead to cognitive and motor disorders. The authors used a basic CNN model to detect Alzheimer's disease in fMRI data [92]. In [93] the authors implemented sparse autoencoders along with scale conjugate gradient to classify the condition of Alzheimer in patients. In [94] the authors made strides in the field of Parkinson's disease detection by using deep CNNs like LeNet and AlexNet.

This is only a tiny snapshot of the large number of medical imaging problems that are being tackled daily by deep learning techniques. More exhaustive literature reviews can be found in [95–98].

1.7 Scope of the book

No doubt, we have wide ranges of medical imaging tools with the use of deep learning models. These models vary based on data complexity and their purposes. In addition to deep learning review and models (see Chapters 2 and 3, respectively), the book provides two different applications: a) Cytology imaging (Chapter 4) and b) COVID-19 prediction, screening, and decision-making (Chapter 5).

References

[1] Alan M. Turing, Computing machinery and intelligence, in: Parsing the Turing Test, Springer, 2009, pp. 23–65.

[2] D.O. Hebb, The organization of behaviour: a neuropsychological study, 1949.

[3] Kevin Warburton, Deep learning and education for sustainability, International Journal of Sustainability in Higher Education 4 (1) (2003) 44–56.

[4] Hyeji Kim, Yihan Jiang, Ranvir Rana, Sreeram Kannan, Sewoong Oh, Pramod Viswanath, Communication algorithms via deep learning, preprint, arXiv:1805.09317, 2018.

[5] Hoang Nguyen, Le-Minh Kieu, Tao Wen, Chen Cai, Deep learning methods in transportation domain: a review, IET Intelligent Transport Systems 12 (9) (2018) 998–1004.

[6] Andreas Kamilaris, Francesc X. Prenafeta-Boldú, Deep learning in agriculture: a survey, Computers and Electronics in Agriculture 147 (2018) 70–90.

[7] James B. Heaton, Nick G. Polson, Jan Hendrik Witte, Deep learning for finance: deep portfolios, Applied Stochastic Models in Business and Industry 33 (1) (2017) 3–12.

[8] Andre Esteva, Alexandre Robicquet, Bharath Ramsundar, Volodymyr Kuleshov, Mark DePristo, Katherine Chou, Claire Cui, Greg Corrado, Sebastian Thrun, Jeff Dean, A guide to deep learning in healthcare, Nature Medicine 25 (1) (2019) 24–29.

[9] KC Santosh, AI-driven tools for coronavirus outbreak: need of active learning and cross-population train/test models on multitudinal/multimodal data, Journal of Medical Systems 44 (5) (2020) 93, https://doi.org/10.1007/s10916-020-01562-1.

[10] Sourodip Ghosh, Ahana Bandyopadhyay, Shreya Sahay, Richik Ghosh, Ishita Kundu, KC Santosh, Colorectal histology tumor detection using ensemble deep neural network, Engineering Applications of Artificial Intelligence 100 (2021) 104202, https://doi.org/10.1016/j.engappai.2021.104202.

[11] Yann LeCun, Léon Bottou, Yoshua Bengio, Patrick Haffner, Gradient-based learning applied to document recognition, Proceedings of the IEEE 86 (11) (1998) 2278–2324.

[12] Geert Litjens, Thijs Kooi, Babak Ehteshami Bejnordi, Arnaud Arindra Adiyoso Setio, Francesco Ciompi, Mohsen Ghafoorian, Jeroen Awm Van Der Laak, Bram Van Ginneken, Clara I. Sánchez, A survey on deep learning in medical image analysis, Medical Image Analysis 42 (2017) 60–88.

[13] KC Santosh, S. Antani, D.S. Guru, N. Dey, Medical Imaging: Artificial Intelligence, Image Recognition, and Machine Learning Techniques, 1st ed., MCRC Press, 2019.

[14] KC Santosh, Sameer K. Antani, Automated chest X-ray screening: can lung region symmetry help detect pulmonary abnormalities?, IEEE Transactions on Medical Imaging 37 (5) (2018) 1168–1177, https://doi.org/10.1109/TMI.2017.2775636.

[15] KC Santosh, Szilárd Vajda, Sameer K. Antani, George R. Thoma, Edge map analysis in chest X-rays for automatic pulmonary abnormality screening, International Journal of Computer Assisted Radiology and Surgery 11 (9) (2016) 1637–1646, https://doi.org/10.1007/s11548-016-1359-6.

[16] Szilárd Vajda, Alexandros Karargyris, Stefan Jäger, KC Santosh, Sema Candemir, Zhiyun Xue, Sameer K. Antani, George R. Thoma, Feature selection for automatic tuberculosis screening in frontal chest radiographs, Journal of Medical Systems 42 (8) (2018) 146, https://doi.org/10.1007/s10916-018-0991-9.

[17] Dipayan Das, KC Santosh, Umapada Pal, Truncated inception net: Covid-19 outbreak screening using chest X-rays, Physical Engineering Sciences in Medicine (8) (2020) 1–11, https://doi.org/10.1007/s13246-020-00888-x.

[18] Alexandros Karargyris, Jenifer Siegelman, Dimitris Tzortzis, Stefan Jaeger, Sema Candemir, Zhiyun Xue, KC Santosh, Szilárd Vajda, Sameer K. Antani, Les R. Folio, George R. Thoma, Combination of texture and shape features to detect pulmonary abnormalities in digital chest X-rays, International Journal of Computer Assisted Radiology and Surgery 11 (1) (2016) 99–106, https://doi.org/10.1007/s11548-015-1242-x.

[19] KC Santosh, Laurent Wendling, Sameer K. Antani, George R. Thoma, Overlaid arrow detection for labeling regions of interest in biomedical images, IEEE Intelligent Systems 31 (3) (2016) 66–75, https://doi.org/10.1109/MIS.2016.24.

[20] KC Santosh, Sema Candemir, Stefan Jäger, Alexandros Karargyris, Sameer K. Antani, George R. Thoma, Les R. Folio, Automatically detecting rotation in chest radiographs using principal rib-orientation measure for quality control, International Journal of Pattern Recognition and Artificial Intelligence 29 (2) (2015) 1557001, https://doi.org/10.1142/S0218001415570013.

[21] KC Santosh, Laurent Wendling, Angular relational signature-based chest radiograph image view classification, Medical & Biological Engineering & Computing 56 (8) (2018) 1447–1458, https://doi.org/10.1007/s11517-018-1786-3.

[22] KC Santosh, Amit Joshi, Covid-19: Prediction, Decision-Making, and Its Impacts, Lecture Notes on Data Engineering and Communications Technologies, 2020.

[23] KC Santosh, Sourodip Ghosh, Covid-19 imaging tools: how big data is big?, Journal of Medical Systems 45 (7) (2021) 71, https://doi.org/10.1007/s10916-021-01747-2.

[24] Amit Joshi, Nilanjan Dey, KC Santosh, Intelligent Systems and Methods to Combat Covid-19, Springer Briefs in Computational Intelligence, 2020.

[25] KC Santosh, COVID-19 prediction models and unexploited data, Journal of Medical Systems 44 (9) (2020) 170, https://doi.org/10.1007/s10916-020-01645-z.

[26] H. Mukherjee, S. Ghosh, A. Dhar, S.M. Obaidullah, KC Santosh, K. Roy, Deep neural network to detect COVID-19: one architecture for both CT scans and chest X-rays, Applied Intelligence 51 (2021) 2777–2789, https://doi.org/10.1007/s10489-020-01943-6.

[27] H. Mukherjee, A. Dhar, S.M. Obaidullah, KC Santosh, K. Roy, Shallow convolutional neural network for Covid-19 outbreak screening using chest X-rays, in: Cognitive Computation, 2021, https://doi.org/10.1007/s12559-020-09775-9.

[28] Tom Michael Mitchell, Machine Learning, McGraw-Hill, 1997.

[29] Leslie Pack Kaelbling, Michael L. Littman, Andrew W. Moore, Reinforcement learning: a survey, Journal of Artificial Intelligence Research 4 (1996) 237–285.

[30] Frederick Hayes-Roth, Rule-based systems, Communications of the ACM 28 (9) (1985) 921–932.

[31] Girish Chandrashekar, Ferat Sahin, A survey on feature selection methods, Computers & Electrical Engineering 40 (1) (2014) 16–28.

[32] Yoshua Bengio, Aaron Courville, Pascal Vincent, Representation learning: a review and new perspectives, IEEE Transactions on Pattern Analysis and Machine Intelligence 35 (8) (2013) 1798–1828.

[33] Mark A. Kramer, Nonlinear principal component analysis using autoassociative neural networks, AIChE Journal 37 (2) (1991) 233–243.

[34] Mark A. Kramer, Autoassociative neural networks, Computers & Chemical Engineering 16 (4) (1992) 313–328.

[35] David E. Rumelhart, Geoffrey E. Hinton, Ronald J. Williams, Learning representations by back-propagating errors, Nature 323 (6088) (1986) 533–536.

[36] Ian Goodfellow, Yoshua Bengio, Aaron Courville, Yoshua Bengio, Deep Learning, vol. 1, MIT Press, Cambridge, 2016.

[37] Yann LeCun, Yoshua Bengio, Geoffrey Hinton, Deep learning, Nature 521 (7553) (2015) 436–444.

[38] Warren S. McCulloch, Walter Pitts, A logical calculus of the ideas immanent in nervous activity, The Bulletin of Mathematical Biophysics 5 (4) (1943) 115–133.

[39] Frank Rosenblatt, The perceptron: a probabilistic model for information storage and organization in the brain, Psychological Review 65 (6) (1958) 386.

[40] Bernard Widrow, et al., Adaptive "adaline" neuron using chemical "memistors", 1960.

[41] J. McCarthy, M. Minsky, N. Rochester, C. Shannon, Dartmouth conference, in: Dartmouth Summer Research Conference on Artificial Intelligence, 1956.

[42] Seymour Papert, Linearly unrecognizable patterns, Mathematical Aspects of Computer Science 19 (1967) 176.

[43] David H. Ackley, Geoffrey E. Hinton, Terrence J. Sejnowski, A learning algorithm for Boltzmann machines, Cognitive Science 9 (1) (1985) 147–169.

[44] Teuvo Kohonen, Self-Organization and Associative Memory, vol. 8, Springer Science & Business Media, 2012.

[45] David H. Hubel, Torsten N. Wiesel, Receptive fields, binocular interaction and functional architecture in the cat's visual cortex, The Journal of Physiology 160 (1) (1962) 106–154.

[46] John J. Hopfield, Neural networks and physical systems with emergent collective computational abilities, Proceedings of the National Academy of Sciences 79 (8) (1982) 2554–2558.

[47] Michael I. Jordan, Attractor dynamics and parallelism in a connectionist sequential machine, in: Artificial Neural Networks: Concept Learning, 1990, pp. 112–127.

[48] Yoshua Bengio, Patrice Simard, Paolo Frasconi, Learning long-term dependencies with gradient descent is difficult, IEEE Transactions on Neural Networks 5 (2) (1994) 157–166.

[49] Sepp Hochreiter, Jürgen Schmidhuber, Long short-term memory, Neural Computation 9 (8) (1997) 1735–1780.

[50] David Kirk, et al., NVIDIA CUDA software and GPU parallel computing architecture, in: ISMM, vol. 7, 2007, pp. 103–104.

[51] Daniel Strigl, Klaus Kofler, Stefan Podlipnig, Performance and scalability of GPU-based convolutional neural networks, in: 2010 18th Euromicro Conference on Parallel, Distributed and Network-Based Processing, IEEE, 2010, pp. 317–324.

[52] Jia Deng, Wei Dong, Richard Socher, Kai Li, Li-Jia Li, Li Fei-Fei, Imagenet: a large-scale hierarchical image database, in: 2009 IEEE Conference on Computer Vision and Pattern Recognition, IEEE, 2009, pp. 248–255.

[53] Sami Abu-El-Haija, Nisarg Kothari, Joonseok Lee, Paul Natsev, George Toderici, Balakrishnan Varadarajan, Sudheendra Vijayanarasimhan, YouTube-8M: a large-scale video classification benchmark, preprint, arXiv: 1609.08675, 2016.

[54] Sinno Jialin Pan, Qiang Yang, A survey on transfer learning, IEEE Transactions on Knowledge and Data Engineering 22 (10) (2009) 1345–1359.

[55] Alex Krizhevsky, Ilya Sutskever, Geoffrey E. Hinton, Imagenet classification with deep convolutional neural networks, in: Advances in Neural Information Processing Systems, 2012, pp. 1097–1105.

[56] A. Berg, J. Deng, L. Fei-Fei, Large scale visual recognition challenge (ILSVRC), http://www.image-net.org/challenges/LSVRC, 2010.

[57] Christian Szegedy, Wei Liu, Yangqing Jia, Pierre Sermanet, Scott Reed, Dragomir Anguelov, Dumitru Erhan, Vincent Vanhoucke, Andrew Rabinovich, Going deeper with convolutions, in: Proceedings of the IEEE Conference on Computer Vision and Pattern Recognition, 2015, pp. 1–9.

[58] Kaiming He, Xiangyu Zhang, Shaoqing Ren, Jian Sun, Deep residual learning for image recognition, in: Proceedings of the IEEE Conference on Computer Vision and Pattern Recognition, 2016, pp. 770–778.

[59] Gao Huang, Zhuang Liu, Laurens Van Der Maaten, Kilian Q. Weinberger, Densely connected convolutional networks, in: Proceedings of the IEEE Conference on Computer Vision and Pattern Recognition, 2017, pp. 4700–4708.

[60] Li Liu, Wanli Ouyang, Xiaogang Wang, Paul Fieguth, Jie Chen, Xinwang Liu, Matti Pietikäinen, Deep learning for generic object detection: a survey, International Journal of Computer Vision 128 (2) (2020) 261–318.

[61] Sandipan Choudhuri, Nibaran Das, Ritesh Sarkhel, Mita Nasipuri, Object localization on natural scenes: a survey, International Journal of Pattern Recognition and Artificial Intelligence 32 (02) (2018) 1855001.

[62] Ross Girshick, Jeff Donahue, Trevor Darrell, Jitendra Malik, Rich feature hierarchies for accurate object detection and semantic segmentation, in: Proceedings of the IEEE Conference on Computer Vision and Pattern Recognition, 2014, pp. 580–587.

[63] Ross Girshick, Fast R-CNN, in: Proceedings of the IEEE International Conference on Computer Vision, 2015, pp. 1440–1448.

[64] Shaoqing Ren, Kaiming He, Ross Girshick, Jian Sun, Faster R-CNN: towards real-time object detection with region proposal networks, in: Advances in Neural Information Processing Systems, 2015, pp. 91–99.

[65] Joseph Redmon, Santosh Divvala, Ross Girshick, Ali Farhadi, You only look once: unified, real-time object detection, in: Proceedings of the IEEE Conference on Computer Vision and Pattern Recognition, 2016, pp. 779–788.

[66] Joseph Redmon, Ali Farhadi, YOLO9000: better, faster, stronger, in: Proceedings of the IEEE Conference on Computer Vision and Pattern Recognition, 2017, pp. 7263–7271.

[67] Joseph Redmon, Ali Farhadi, Yolov3: an incremental improvement, preprint, arXiv:1804.02767, 2018.

[68] Swarnendu Ghosh, Nibaran Das, Ishita Das, Ujjwal Maulik, Understanding deep learning techniques for image segmentation, ACM Computing Surveys (CSUR) 52 (4) (2019) 1–35.

[69] Swarnendu Ghosh, Anisha Pal, Shourya Jaiswal, KC Santosh, Nibaran Das, Mita Nasipuri, SegFast-V2: semantic image segmentation with less parameters in deep learning for autonomous driving, International Journal of Machine Learning and Cybernetics 10 (11) (2019) 3145–3154.

[70] Vijay Badrinarayanan, Alex Kendall, Roberto Cipolla, Segnet: a deep convolutional encoder-decoder architecture for image segmentation, IEEE Transactions on Pattern Analysis and Machine Intelligence 39 (12) (2017) 2481–2495.

[71] Olaf Ronneberger, Philipp Fischer, Thomas Brox, U-net: convolutional networks for biomedical image segmentation, in: International Conference on Medical Image Computing and Computer-Assisted Intervention, Springer, 2015, pp. 234–241.

[72] M.D. Zakir Hossain, Ferdous Sohel, Mohd Fairuz Shiratuddin, Hamid Laga, A comprehensive survey of deep learning for image captioning, ACM Computing Surveys (CSUR) 51 (6) (2019) 1–36.

[73] Qi Wu, Damien Teney, Peng Wang, Chunhua Shen, Anthony Dick, Anton van den Hengel, Visual question answering: a survey of methods and datasets, Computer Vision and Image Understanding 163 (2017) 21–40.

[74] Shantanu Kumar, A survey of deep learning methods for relation extraction, preprint, arXiv:1705.03645, 2017.

[75] Samitha Herath, Mehrtash Harandi, Fatih Porikli, Going deeper into action recognition: a survey, Image and Vision Computing 60 (2017) 4–21.

[76] Kyunghyun Cho, Bart Van Merriënboer, Caglar Gulcehre, Dzmitry Bahdanau, Fethi Bougares, Holger Schwenk, Yoshua Bengio, Learning phrase representations using RNN encoder-decoder for statistical machine translation, preprint, arXiv:1406.1078, 2014.

[77] Palash Goyal, Emilio Ferrara, Graph embedding techniques, applications, and performance: a survey, Knowledge-Based Systems 151 (2018) 78–94.

[78] Ji Wan, Dayong Wang, Steven Chu Hong Hoi, Pengcheng Wu, Jianke Zhu, Yongdong Zhang, Jintao Li, Deep learning for content-based image retrieval: a comprehensive study, in: Proceedings of the 22nd ACM International Conference on Multimedia, 2014, pp. 157–166.

[79] Daniel W. Otter, Julian R. Medina, Jugal K. Kalita, A survey of the usages of deep learning for natural language processing, IEEE Transactions on Neural Networks and Learning Systems (2020).

[80] Varun Gulshan, Lily Peng, Marc Coram, Martin C. Stumpe, Derek Wu, Arunachalam Narayanaswamy, Subhashini Venugopalan, Kasumi Widner, Tom Madams, Jorge Cuadros, et al., Development and validation of a deep learning algorithm for detection of diabetic retinopathy in retinal fundus photographs, JAMA 316 (22) (2016) 2402–2410.

[81] T. Chandrakumar, R. Kathirvel, Classifying diabetic retinopathy using deep learning architecture, International Journal of Engineering Research & Technology 5 (6) (2016) 19–24.

[82] Korsuk Sirinukunwattana, Shan E. Ahmed Raza, Yee-Wah Tsang, David R.J. Snead, Ian A. Cree, Nasir M. Rajpoot, Locality sensitive deep learning for detection and classification of nuclei in routine colon cancer histology images, IEEE Transactions on Medical Imaging 35 (5) (2016) 1196–1206.

[83] Neslihan Bayramoglu, Janne Heikkilä, Transfer learning for cell nuclei classification in histopathology images, in: European Conference on Computer Vision, Springer, 2016, pp. 532–539.

[84] John A. Quinn, Rose Nakasi, Pius K.B. Mugagga, Patrick Byanyima, William Lubega, Alfred Andama, Deep convolutional neural networks for microscopy-based point of care diagnostics, in: Machine Learning for Healthcare Conference, 2016, pp. 271–281.

[85] Xiao Jia, Max Q.-H. Meng, A deep convolutional neural network for bleeding detection in wireless capsule endoscopy images, in: 2016 38th Annual International Conference of the IEEE Engineering in Medicine and Biology Society (EMBC), IEEE, 2016, pp. 639–642.

[86] Panpeng Li, Ziyun Li, Fei Gao, Li Wan, Jun Yu, Convolutional neural networks for intestinal hemorrhage detection in wireless capsule endoscopy images, in: 2017 IEEE International Conference on Multimedia and Expo (ICME), IEEE, 2017, pp. 1518–1523.

[87] Romain Leenhardt, Pauline Vasseur, Cynthia Li, Jean Christophe Saurin, Gabriel Rahmi, Franck Cholet, Aymeric Becq, Philippe Marteau, Aymeric Histace, Xavier Dray, et al., A neural network algorithm for detection of GI angiectasia during small-bowel capsule endoscopy, Gastrointestinal Endoscopy 89 (1) (2019) 189–194.

[88] Gregor Urban, Priyam Tripathi, Talal Alkayali, Mohit Mittal, Farid Jalali, William Karnes, Pierre Baldi, Deep learning localizes and identifies polyps in real time with 96% accuracy in screening colonoscopy, Gastroenterology 155 (4) (2018) 1069–1078.

[89] Geert Litjens, Francesco Ciompi, Jelmer M. Wolterink, Bob D. de Vos, Tim Leiner, Jonas Teuwen, Ivana Išgum, State-of-the-art deep learning in cardiovascular image analysis, JACC: Cardiovascular Imaging 12 (8) (2019) 1549–1565.

[90] Zhiqiong Wang, Ge Yu, Yan Kang, Yingjie Zhao, Qixun Qu, Breast tumor detection in digital mammography based on extreme learning machine, Neurocomputing 128 (2014) 175–184.

[91] Li Shen, Laurie R. Margolies, Joseph H. Rothstein, Eugene Fluder, Russell McBride, Weiva Sieh, Deep learning to improve breast cancer detection on screening mammography, Scientific Reports 9 (1) (2019) 1–12.

[92] Saman Sarraf, Ghassem Tofighi, Alzheimer's Disease Neuroimaging Initiative, et al., Deepad: Alzheimer's disease classification via deep convolutional neural networks using MRI and fMRI, BioRxiv (2016) 070441.

[93] Debesh Jha, G. Kwon, Alzheimer's disease detection using sparse autoencoder, scale conjugate gradient and softmax output layer with fine tuning, International Journal of Machine Learning and Computing 7 (1) (2017) 13–17.

[94] Andrés Ortiz, Jorge Munilla, Manuel Martínez, Juan Manuel Gorriz, Javier Ramírez, Diego Salas-Gonzalez, Parkinson's disease detection using isosurfaces-based features and convolutional neural networks, Frontiers in Neuroinformatics 13 (2019) 48.

[95] Dinggang Shen, Guorong Wu, Heung-Il Suk, Deep learning in medical image analysis, Annual Review of Biomedical Engineering 19 (2017) 221–248.

[96] Daniele Ravì, Charence Wong, Fani Deligianni, Melissa Berthelot, Javier Andreu-Perez, Benny Lo, Guang-Zhong Yang, Deep learning for health informatics, IEEE Journal of Biomedical and Health Informatics 21 (1) (2016) 4–21.

[97] Xiaoxuan Liu, Livia Faes, Aditya U. Kale, Siegfried K. Wagner, Dun Jack Fu, Alice Bruynseels, Thushika Mahendiran, Gabriella Moraes, Mohith Shamdas, Christoph Kern, et al., A comparison of deep learning performance against health-care professionals in detecting diseases from medical imaging: a systematic review and meta-analysis, The Lancet Digital Health 1 (6) (2019) e271–e297.

[98] Mainak Biswas, Venkatanareshbabu Kuppili, Luca Saba, Damodar Reddy Edla, Harman S. Suri, Elisa Cuadrado-Godia, John R. Laird, Rui Tato Marinhoe, Joao M. Sanches, Andrew Nicolaides, et al., State-of-the-art review on deep learning in medical imaging, Frontiers in Bioscience (Landmark Edition) 24 (2019) 392–426.

CHAPTER 2

Deep learning: a review

2.1 Background

The term "deep learning" has become one of the most commonly used terms in the field of machine learning during the last decade. However, the concepts that led to this field date back to the introduction of the first neuron by McCullough and Pitts. Since then, it has been a rough road for neural learning systems. The history of neural learning systems was scarred with some major setbacks. With the initial proposition of artificial neurons by McCulloch and Pitts [1] and the introduction Hebbian learning systems [2], the cybernetics era kicked off. The proposed model of perceptron [3] could simulate linear models with learnable weights. Adaptive linear units (ADALINE) [4] with gradient-based learning principle set the foundation of modern neural networks. But the limitation of linear systems soon crept up as they were found unable to learn cases with dependent variables like in case of the XOR problem [5]. It took almost a decade before multilayer models started to arrive since the introduction of the Neocognitron [6,7], a hierarchical self-organizing neural architecture. The idea was based on the works of Hubel and Wiesel [8] on the striate cortex of a cat that showed the multilayer nature of the visual cortex. However, the problem extended the idea of stochastic gradient-based learning over multiple layers. That is when the idea of back-propagation [9] surfaced. With back-propagation the error from the visible layers could be propagated as a chain of partial derivatives to the weights in the intermediate layers. Introduction of nonlinear activation functions such as sigmoid units allowed these intermediate gradients to flow without break and solve the XOR problem. Although it was clear that deeper networks provided better learning capability, they also induce vanishing or exploding gradients [10]. This was the second major setback in the evolution of neural learning systems that lasted until long short-term memory cells were proposed to replace traditional recurrent neural networks. Further down a decade the deep learning era started with Hinton proposing the restricted Boltzmann machines [11] and the deep belief networks [12], where layerwise training allowed deeper networks to be trained.

Needless to say that we have, in the literature, several different deep learning architectures for different purposes. Medical imaging is no exception. A few of them can be categorized in terms of their objectives, such as pulmonary abnormality screening [13–17]; segmentation (or region-of-interest selection) [18,19], and image view classification (e.g., chest X-rays [20]) and tumor detection [21]. Within the scope, we can also consider COVID-19 screening, where different models were employed for prediction, screening, and decision-making processes [16,22–29]. In this chapter, instead of focusing on medical imaging tools, we provide a comprehensive review of deep learning models/architectures.

2.2 Artificial neural networks

As the name suggests, artificial neural networks draw inspiration from the biological counterparts. The human brain is composed of a huge number of neurons that create a network. The neurons work by generating electrical impulses by manipulating the difference between ion potentials inside and outside the body of the neuron. When a significant potential difference is achieved, an impulse or spike is generated. The neurons have two main parts, dendron and axon. The axon of one neuron is connected to the dendron of another neuron by means of a synapse. The spike allows a neuron to release particles called neurotransmitters through these synapses, which is then passed on to the dendron of the subsequent neuron. A chain of neurons passing on information to one another creates a spike train that is mainly responsible for all our cognitive functions. A spike train is usually initiated by a receptor based on some stimuli, which passes through the neural network and creates an appropriate response by firing another spike train aimed at the necessary effector.

An artificial neuron is a mathematical model [1] that simulates a similar methodology to mimic a decision-making process based on a series of inputs.

2.2.1 The neuron

The study of deep learning starts from the understanding of a single decision-making element called a neuron. As shown in Fig. 2.1, a neuron produces a scalar output based on a unit vector. The behavior of a neuron is defined by a set of weights that control the flow of information from each input element, and a decision is taken using an activation function. Each neuron models a hyperplane in the input space that serves as a decision boundary dividing the input space into two regions. The goal of "training" a neuron is to define a set of weights such that the corresponding decision boundary serves a logical separator able to distinguish between two categories of samples.

Let us consider an m-dimensional input vector $\mathbf{x}$, where $x_1, x_2, \ldots, x_m$ are the input signals. A neuron with m synaptic weights defined by $\mathbf{w} = w_1, w_2, \ldots, w_m$ can accept such a set of input signals. Each of the synaptic weights is multiplied by the corresponding input signal. The weights alter the values of the signals to control how much each signal contributes toward the output. As shown in Fig. 2.2, whereas the set of weights control the angle of the hyperplane,

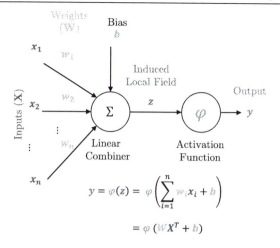

$$y = \varphi(z) = \varphi\left(\sum_{i=1}^{n} w_i x_i + b\right)$$

$$= \varphi\left(WX^T + b\right)$$

Figure 2.1: A graphical representation of the artificial neuron.

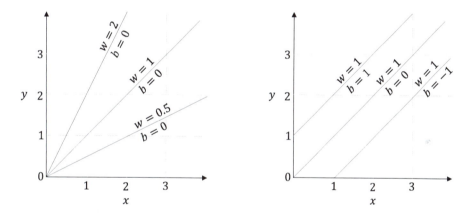

Figure 2.2: Effect of weights and bias of a neuron on the corresponding hyperplane.

its position or axis intercept is defined by a bias value b. The weighted input signals and the bias are summed to create an induced local field or an activation potential v. This can be represented as

$$z = \sum_{i=1}^{m} w_i x_i + b. \tag{2.1}$$

An activation function ϕ acts a decision function that accepts the activation potential outputs a signal demonstrating if the neuron is activated or not. The output signal is defined as

$$y = \varphi(z). \tag{2.2}$$

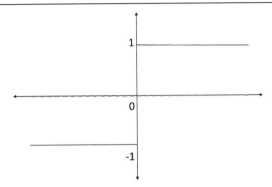

Figure 2.3: The plot of a signum function.

2.2.2 Activation functions

The activation function φ is the decision-making element that defines the decision boundary in the input space by setting a threshold in the induced local field. Without an activation function, the output signal becomes a simple linear function. As we know, linear functions are only single-grade polynomials that render the neuron to act as a linear regression model. No matter how many linear functions we stack, we will always get a linear function as an output. Hence activation of the linear combiner enables us to create complex decision boundaries by using a combination of multiple neurons.

The simplest activation function can be defined by a step function

$$\varphi(z) = \begin{cases} 1 & \text{if } z \geq 0, \\ 0 & \text{if } z < 0, \end{cases} \tag{2.3}$$

where z is the induced local field as defined in Eq. (2.1). The step function can be modified to output values among $1, 0$ and -1 by implementing the signum function (see Fig. 2.3)

$$\varphi(z) = \begin{cases} 1 & \text{if } z > 0, \\ 0 & \text{if } z = 0, \\ -1 & \text{if } z < 0. \end{cases} \tag{2.4}$$

Although a threshold based decision function serves its purpose as a binary classifier, it is hard to train. If a neuron only provides positive or negative output, then it loses a lot of information regarding the strength of the activation. It would be easier to approximate a complex boundary by a combination of neurons if the strength of activation of each neuron is somehow depicted. Not only is it necessary to easily model a complex nonlinear decision boundary, but

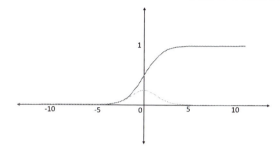

Figure 2.4: Sigmoid activation function (red) and its derivative (green dashed).

the training protocol for neural networks also benefits from a function with nonzero gradients. Neural networks are trained by a gradient-based iterative optimization technique called back-propagation (will be discussed later). The sign function has a gradient of zero for all real numbers other than zero and hence is not suitable for performing gradient-based optimization. This is where nonlinear activation functions come into play.

One of the most commonly used nonlinear activation functions is the sigmoid function

$$\sigma(z) = \frac{1}{1 + e^{-z}}. \tag{2.5}$$

The sigmoid function shown in Fig. 2.4 has some nice properties. Firstly, it presents a softer version of the signum function and thus serves as a gradient-friendly alternative to the standard binary classifier. The gradient is steep around zero and flattens as it moves farther away on either side. The output has a nice bound between 0 and 1. This allows the optimizer to update the weights in a way so that the output of the neuron is pushed toward either 0 or 1. Another benefit of using a sigmoid function is that its derivative can be easily expressed in terms of itself as follows:

$$\sigma'(z) = \sigma(z)(1 - \sigma(z)). \tag{2.6}$$

If the output of a neuron is desired to be bounded between -1 and 1, then the tan hyperbolic (tanh) activation function (see Fig. 2.5) can be used. Like the sigmoid function, the tanh function also has the same features except that it is bounded between -1 and 1 and not between 0 and 1 like the sigmoid. The tanh function and its derivative can be expressed as

$$\tanh(z) = \frac{e^z - e^{-z}}{e^z + e^{-z}} \quad \text{and} \tag{2.7}$$

$$\tanh'(z) = 1 - \tanh^2(z). \tag{2.8}$$

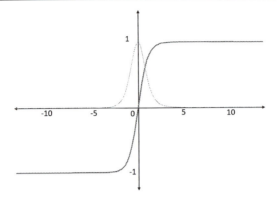

Figure 2.5: Tanh activation function (red) and its derivative (green dashed).

Sigmoid and tanh functions work well as approximation functions for classification purpose, but in a network with lots of neurons the nature of activation is pretty dense. These activation functions provide analog signals, and effectively all neurons in a network fire some amount of signal for every sample. This is very inefficient in terms of representation. Furthermore, the values of gradients are generally fractional in nature bounded by unity. Therefore, when stacking multiple layers of such neurons, they contribute as a diminishing factor to the chain of local derivatives. The standard training protocol for neural networks, known as back-propagation, expresses the global gradient of an objective with respect to weight as this chain of local derivatives. By successive multiplication of such fractional derivatives the gradient can often vanish across large depths. To address these issues, the rectified linear unit or ReLU activation function was proposed [30]:

$$relu(z) = \max(0, z). \qquad (2.9)$$

The basis of relu is incorporating nonlinearity in the standard linear activation function. The linear activation function has a nice property that the gradient is 1. Hence the chain of partial derivatives is not affected by any diminishing factors. However, unlike the linear function, the ReLU forces all negative values to zeros as shown in Fig. 2.6. This serves two purposes. Firstly, it folds the feature space by shifting all negative activation to zero, thus enforcing non-linearity. Secondly, in a large network, many neurons output a zero activation, thus bringing sparsity in the system [31]. Sparse systems are more efficient as they are less computationally expensive and also avoid overfitting (discussed later). For activations in the negative regions of ReLu, the gradient is 0 because of which the weights will not get updated during training. That means, those neurons which go into that state will stop responding to variations in error. This is called the dying ReLu problem. A simple fix to this problem is allowing a small constant gradient in the negative zone to allow the weights to recover if necessary. This is called a

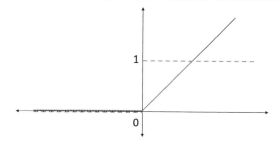

Figure 2.6: Rectified linear units (red) and its derivative (green dashed).

leaky relu and is defined by

$$\text{LeakyRELU}(z) = \begin{cases} z & \text{if } z > 0, \\ \alpha z & \text{otherwise,} \end{cases} \tag{2.10}$$

where α is generally a small value.

2.2.3 Multilayer feed forward neural network

A single neuron can model an $(n-1)$-dimensional hyperplane in an n-dimensional space. To model more complex functions, multiple neurons are required to work together. Whereas neurons with linear activations can be combined, the output will always be a linear hyperplane irrespective of the number of neurons or their arrangement. Hence nonlinear activations are necessary to model complex functions.

Multilayer neural networks [11] are proposed to address this factor. A multilayer feed-forward neural network consists of multiple neurons arranged in layers where neurons of each layer accept a vector of input signals and provide an output. The outputs of all the neurons in this layer serve as the input vector for the next layer. These layers of neurons can be of two types, the visible layer and the hidden layer. The visible layer, also known as the output layer, is the last layer of the network that is exposed directly to the error gradient. All the previous layers are hidden from the desired output and hence known as hidden layers. A structure of a multilayer feed forward is demonstrated in Fig. 2.7.

Theoretically, a neural network with a single hidden layer is enough to approximate any continuous functions on compact subsets of $\mathbb{R}^n$. This is established by the universal approximation which goes as follows.

Universal approximation theorem: Let $\varphi : \mathbb{R} \to \mathbb{R}$ be a nonconstant, bounded, and continuous function (called the activation function). Let I_m denote the m-dimensional unit hypercube $[0, 1]^m$. The space of real-valued continuous functions on I_m is denoted by $C(I_m)$.

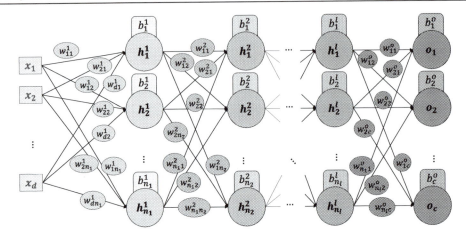

Figure 2.7: A detailed depiction of a multilayered perceptron (MLP).

Then, given any $\varepsilon > 0$ and any function $f \in C(I_m)$, there exist an integer N, real constants $v_i, b_i \in \mathbb{R}$, and real vectors $w_i \in \mathbb{R}^m$ for $i = 1, \ldots, N$ such that we may define

$$F(x) = \sum_{i=1}^{N} v_i \varphi \left(w_i^T x + b_i \right) \tag{2.11}$$

as an approximate realization of the function f, that is,

$$|F(x) - f(x)| < \varepsilon \tag{2.12}$$

for all $x \in I_m$. In other words, the functions of the form $F(x)$ are dense in $C(I_m)$. This still holds when I_m is replaced with any compact subset of $\mathbb{R}^m$.

Although a single layer may be enough to approximate a large number of problems, it is not the most efficient alternative. Imagine a classifier distinguishing between 3 objects, say a house, a truck, and a ball. Each of the objects can have 3 colors, say red, yellow, and blue. Now there exist 9 possible variations with these 3 objects and 3 colors. So for a single-layer neural network to effectively recognize each category, we need 9 neurons. However, the same concept can be modeled by two separate layers of neurons, where one layer has 3 neurons corresponding to each color,and another has 3 neurons corresponding to each object. The same concept can be represented by using only 6 neurons. The increased depth of the network allowed the model to remove redundancy by separating independent concepts. For the same level of performance, deeper networks can be much more efficient than wider networks [12]. This is why deep learning techniques perform so well for complex real-world problems. Its depth allows the model to approximate extremely complex hyperplanes and recognize high-level complex features by successively combining low-level redundant concepts.

2.2.4 Training neural networks by back-propagation

Previously, we have seen how a single neuron models a decision boundary. A neuron is defined by a set of weights and biases that enables the neuron to fire a positive response based on certain input signals. The values of these weights and biases define the position and orientation of the hyperplane. Any weight w or bias b of a neuron can be optimized by a very simple gradient base update rule given by

$$w = w - \eta \frac{dE}{dw}, \tag{2.13}$$

$$b = b - \eta \frac{dE}{db}, \tag{2.14}$$

where E is an error function that computes the difference between the observed and desired outputs. The error gradient dE/dw is indicative of the change in the error with respect to the change in the weight. We would like to follow along the negative slope of the gradient to reach a minimum error value. The learning rate η controls the amount by which the weights are updated so that the training can progress at a brisk pace but not too much as to overshoot the local minima. To compute the gradient, let us consider a neuron that takes an input vector $\mathbf{x}$, multiplies it by weights denoted by $\mathbf{w}$, and passes it to a linear combiner along with a bias b. The output of the linear combiner z is then passed through an activation function φ, and the final activated output y is received. A neuron indexed by n can be written as

$$y_n = \varphi(z_n) \tag{2.15}$$

$$= \varphi \left(\sum_i w_i^n x_i + b^n \right), \tag{2.16}$$

where w_i^n refers to the weight corresponding neuron n, the ith component of the input vector is given by x_i, and b^n is the bias. The error function E computes the difference between the observed output y_n and desired output $\hat{y}_n$. The gradient dE/dw_i^n can be expressed as

$$\frac{\delta E}{\delta w_j^n} = \frac{\delta E}{\delta y_n} \frac{\delta y_n}{\delta z_n} \frac{\delta z_n}{\delta w_j^n}. \tag{2.17}$$

This chain of derivatives represents three components, the local error gradient in the output layer $\delta E/\delta y_n$, the local gradient of the activation function $\delta y_n/\delta z_n$, and the local gradient of the linear combiner $\delta z_n/\delta w_j^n$.

The same idea can be implemented for multilayer feed forward networks, as graphically shown in Fig. 2.8. A multilayered feed forward network is defined as multiple neuron cascades of layers, where outputs of each layer of neurons are combined to form the input vector

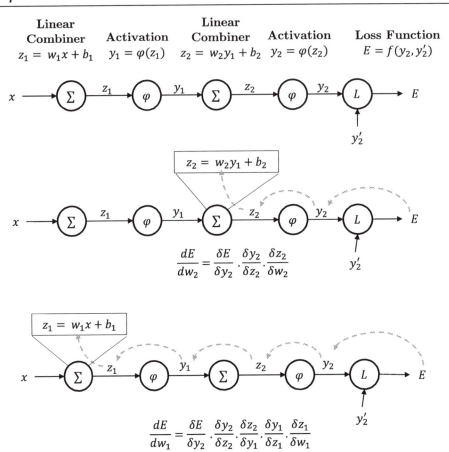

Figure 2.8: Long distance gradients as a chain of partial derivatives.

for the following layer of neurons. All neurons in a layer receive the same input vector but have their distinct sets of weights. An input signal passes through such multiple layers before reaching the output layer. If each layer is treated as functions $f_1, f_2, \dots f_n$, then the error gradient with respect to the kth weight in layer i can be written as

$$\frac{\delta E}{\delta w_k^i} = \frac{\delta E}{\delta f_n} \frac{\delta f_n}{\delta f_{n-1}} \frac{\delta f_{n-1}}{\delta f_{n-2}} \dots \frac{\delta f_{i+1}}{\delta f_i} \frac{\delta f_i}{\delta w_k^i}. \tag{2.18}$$

This representation of global gradients as a backward propagating chain of local gradients is called the back-propagation algorithm. For a back-propagation algorithm [9] to work, it must be ensured that all the functions in the computational graphs have derivatives at all points. Note that the depth of the network has a significant impact on the length of the derivative chain, and hence the value of local derivatives must be regulated carefully. Otherwise, product of too many values can cause the gradient to explode or vanish.

2.2.5 Optimization

As discussed previously, the weights $\mathbf{w}_n$ and biases $\mathbf{b}_n$ of every neuron n in a neural network N control the overall output y. So for any change in the weights and biases, the output will also change:

$$\forall n \in N, \mathbf{w}_n + \Delta \mathbf{w}_n \implies y + \Delta y, \text{ and} \tag{2.19}$$

$$b_n + \Delta b_n \implies y + \Delta y. \tag{2.20}$$

The goal of the training process is finding the optimal update in weight, such that a relevant error E is reduced. In Section 2.2.4, we have seen how with we can update weights and biases with back-propagation by computing the gradient of the error with respect to weights and biases.

2.2.5.1 Objective functions

Optimization problems are often addressed in terms of an objective function or criterion that is used to find a candidate solution. Depending on the problem, we may desire to maximize or minimize an objective function. As discussed previously, neural networks are trained by updating the weights of the network so that a relevant error is minimized. An objective function designed to find out the error of a complex system is called a loss function. Loss functions are also sometimes referred to as cost functions or error functions. The purpose of a loss function in a neural network is reducing a complex output by a system to a single scalar value that signifies its difference from the desired output. Depending on the problem, there can be several kinds of loss functions. We discuss some popular loss functions.

Mean squared error

An outright difference between the observed tensor and a desired tensor can serve as a viable loss function. It is one of the most commonly sought methods for regression problems. A squared error between the m-dimensional observed vector $\mathbf{y}$ and desired vector $\mathbf{y}'$ is given as

$$E_{MSE} = \frac{1}{m} \sum_{i=1}^{m} (y_i - \hat{y}_i)^2. \tag{2.21}$$

Although the mean squared error is extremely suitable for regression problems, it is somewhat inefficient for classification problem. If we compute the gradient of the mean squared error with respect to weights or biases, then we will see

$$\frac{\delta E}{\delta w} = \frac{1}{m} \sum_{i=1}^{m} \left(\frac{\delta}{\delta w} (y_i - \hat{y}_i)^2 \right) \qquad (2.22)$$

$$= \frac{2}{m} \sum_{i=1}^{m} \left(\frac{\delta y_i}{\delta w} \right). \qquad (2.23)$$

The actual value of the error has no effect on the gradient, and hence the network will learn at the same pace irrelevant of the fact how far it is from the optimal solution.

Cross-entropy measures

For discriminative learning problems like classification, entropy-based functions are much more efficient. A binary classification can be carried out by any network that learns a binomial distribution. A binary cross-entropy error (E_{BCE}) between the observed output y and the desired output $\hat{y}$ is given as

$$E_{BCE} = - \left(\hat{y} \log y + (1 - \hat{y}) \log(1 - y) \right). \qquad (2.24)$$

Since this is a binary classification task, $\hat{y} \in \{0, 1\}$. Due to the nature of the logarithmic curve, we see that the error tends to infinity as y moves away from $\hat{y}$. Compute the gradient, we find

$$\frac{\delta E}{\delta w} = \frac{\delta}{\delta w} (- \left(\hat{y} \log y + (1 - \hat{y}) \log(1 - y) \right)) \qquad (2.25)$$

$$= - \left(\frac{\hat{y}}{y} \frac{\delta y}{\delta w} - \frac{1 - \hat{y}}{1 - y} \frac{\delta y}{\delta w} \right) \qquad (2.26)$$

$$= \frac{\delta y}{\delta w} \frac{y - \hat{y}}{y(1 - y)}. \qquad (2.27)$$

As apparent from this equation, the steepness of the error gradient is directly proportional to $y - \hat{y}$, which is the difference between the observed and desired values. This makes cross-entropy measures much more effective loss functions for classification tasks. The binary cross entropy error formula can be extended to a categorical cross entropy function E_{CCE} for multiclass classification:

$$E_{CCE} = - \sum_{i=1}^{C} \hat{y}_i \log y_i. \qquad (2.28)$$

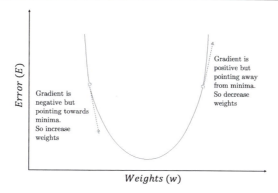

Figure 2.9: The idea behind stochastic gradient descent (SGD).

If only one correct class exists, then all the other corresponding elements of the summation become zero, and we can represent the categorical cross entropy error as a negative log likelihood of the correct class:

$$E_{NLL} = -\log(y_c), \tag{2.29}$$

where y_c is the output corresponding to the correct class. For problems with large number of classes, this makes the computation of the loss function extremely efficient.

2.2.5.2 Optimization techniques

A neural network is trained by exposing it to multiple number of training samples. The output of the network is compared to a predefined desired set of values, and a relevant loss function is minimized. The performance of a neural network greatly depends on the amount and quality of training samples. Several challenges are associated with the training process. The surface of the loss function in the weight space plays a significant role. Various factors like local minima, saddle points, cliffs, and so on can affect the training process to a great extent. The standard training procedure for weight update is called a stochastic gradient descent, which depends on the loss surface (see Fig. 2.9).

Stochastic gradient descent

The stochastic gradient descent [32] updates the weights based on the error gradient:

$$w = w - \eta \frac{dE}{dw}. \tag{2.30}$$

The most straightforward way to implement this is to pass one sample through the network, compute the error, calculate the gradients, and then update the weights. This is in concordance with standard optimization protocol. However, in machine learning a statistically sound

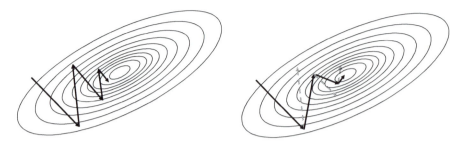

Figure 2.10: Effect of momentum on learning: The red dashed line represents the direction of the supposed update in the absence of momentum.

approach is to consider high number of training samples to reduce uncertainty. This can be achieved by calculating a combined error on all training samples and finding a resultant gradient, which is a much better option for a globally acceptable weight update. Weight updates due to single samples can be erratic. However, a gradient corresponding to a combined error over all samples more updates the weight in a much more appropriate direction. This is known as batch gradient descent.

Even though this is theoretically more acceptable, the computational overhead increases significantly for a higher number of samples, which is less than linear returns. A middle ground to both is the method considering a mini-batch stochastic gradient descent, where the loss is computed over a small batch of samples, thus preventing weight updates from being too erratic and keeping the process computationally manageable at the same time.

Momentum

The shape of gradient contours plays an important role in the efficiency of stochastic gradient descent. High curvatures in the contours can cause gradients to move in inefficient zig-zags perpendicular to the slope of the gradient. Inspired by the physics of a rolling ball, [33] came up with the idea of "momentum". The concept of "momentum" states that the previous gradients have a decaying impact on the current gradient. This impact of previous gradients reduces opposing components and forces the weight to move faster down the slope as shown in Fig. 2.10. The weight updating protocol is defined as

$$\mathbf{v} = \alpha\mathbf{v} - \eta\frac{dE}{dw}, \tag{2.31}$$

$$w = w + \mathbf{v}, \tag{2.32}$$

where α is a coefficient that controls the decay of impact of previous gradients, and $\mathbf{v}$ is the updated gradient with added momentum.

Adaptive learning rates

Although the momentum increases the speed of learning, it is also necessary to put a check on the learning rate so that the weights do not overshoot the optimal value. The learning rate η acts as a coefficient for the gradient by reducing it to change the weights in smaller steps. A high learning rate will change the weights by a large value, and this may make them overshoot the local minima. However, too small minima will make the process of training extremely long. Hence it is advisable to start with high learning rate and slowly reduce the value as the weight approaches the local minimum. This can be either done manually with a learning rate scheduler that reduces the learning rate by a predefined factor after certain number of iterations over the dataset or by automatic methods [34] like RMSProp or adaptive moments (Adam) [35].

2.2.6 Regularization

Machine learning problems are fundamentally built to perform intelligent tasks on unseen samples. When it comes to neural networks, a large number of samples with similar input distribution is the challenge to be addressed. However, the generalization capability of the network defines its ability to perform well on unseen samples. Regularization is defined as any method that enhances the generalization capability of a network.

Overfitting

In standard training protocol a neural network is fed with a bunch of training samples, and the weights are updated to minimize the output of a loss function. To check the performance of the network, a validation set is used, which is composed of samples that the network has not been exposed to during the training routine. Various hyperparameters of the network, such as number of neurons, layers, activation functions, number of iterations, and so on, can be changed to make the network perform on this validation set. Finally, the performance of the network is reported on the test set, which is a fresh batch of unseen samples.

For a correctly initialized network, the training performance and the validation performance start to improve as the training starts. However, as shown in Fig. 2.11, it is often seen that after sometime the validation performance becomes stagnant or even becomes worse though the training performance keeps on increasing. This is called overfitting [36]. As the network tries to approximate the decision boundary, a point is reached when the boundary becomes so tightly bound to the training samples that it starts predicting the unseen samples wrongly.

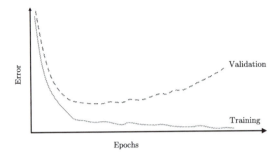

Figure 2.11: Error curve showing overfitting.

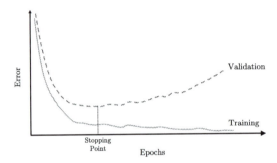

Figure 2.12: Early stopping: Stopping the training procedure at the point of minimum validation error.

Regularization strategies

This difference between the training performance and the validation performance is known as a generalization error. Various regularization techniques can be applied to reduce this generalization error without compromising the overall performance. The generic goal of a regularization technique is to restrain the network from converging at the absolute minimum of the training error space. If the absolute minimum of the training error is reached, there is a chance that some concepts that are learned are solely tuned toward specific training samples and will not be applicable for unseen samples. So by restraining the network from reaching the minimum this phenomenon is avoided. We discuss some common methods for regularization.

1) *Early stopping*

As mentioned below, a validation set contains samples to which network has not been trained with. These samples can be used to check the performance of the network on unseen data. Plotting the performance of the network on the training and validation set for every iteration over the dataset, we can find out the optimal number of iterations for which the validation performance is the best. This knowledge can be used to stop the training before overfitting begins [37] (Fig. 2.12).

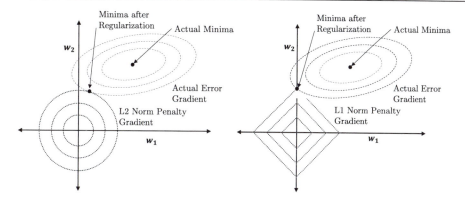

Figure 2.13: Parameter norm penalties: $L2$ norm regularization (left) and $L1$ norm regularization (right).

2) *Parameter norm penalties*

Parameter norm penalties or weight decay [38] act as a secondary objective that pulls the network away from reaching the absolute minimum of the error gradient. This prevents the network from overfitting the training samples. As shown in Fig. 2.13, the modified objective function contains an additional component that forces the weights to be nearer to the origin. Depending on the requirement, this can be achieved by reducing a norm of the weight vector along with the actual objective. For a network with parameters $\mathbf{w}$, which is trained on training samples $\mathbf{X}$ and ground truth $\mathbf{y}$, let the standard objective function be defined by $J(\mathbf{w}; \mathbf{X}, \mathbf{y})$. There are two ways of implementing parameter norm penalties for regularization.

a) $L1$ regularization: $L1$ norm regularization implements a technique called lasso regression, which adds the absolute values of the weights as a penalty term to the loss function. The updated loss function J_{L1} is given by

$$J_{L1}(\mathbf{w}; \mathbf{X}, \mathbf{y}) = J_{L1}(\mathbf{w}; \mathbf{X}, \mathbf{y}) + \lambda \sum_{i} |w_i|, \qquad (2.33)$$

where λ is a coefficient that controls the effect of regularization. $L1$ regularization forces various components of the weight vector to become zero. This is particularly useful when sparsity is desired in the weight vectors.

b) $L1$ regularization: $L2$ norm regularization implements ridge regression that adds the squared values of the weights as a penalty term to the loss function. The updated loss function J_{L1} is given by

$$J_{L1}(\mathbf{w}; \mathbf{X}, \mathbf{y}) = J_{L1}(\mathbf{w}; \mathbf{X}, \mathbf{y}) + \lambda \sum_{i} w_i^2, \qquad (2.34)$$

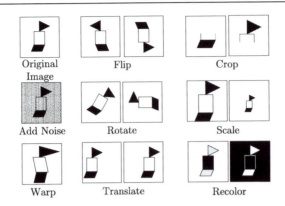

Figure 2.14: Different types of data augmentation.

where λ is a coefficient that controls the effect of regularization. *L2* regularization forces various components of the weight vector to be close to the origin.

In either case, because of the norm penalty in the loss functions, the weights are prevented to reach the minimum of training error surface, thus avoiding the network from overfitting the training samples.

3) *Augmentation*

Neural networks thrive on the variety of the training samples provided. However, collection and annotation of training data can be infeasible in various circumstances. In these cases the neural network can fail to learn generic concepts that model variations in the input space. Augmentation is a way to mimic this variation [39]. It is achieved by altering input samples in a controlled environment so that these variations can be simulated. As shown in Fig. 2.14, data augmentation can be carried out in various ways [40]. For example, in a dataset of images of different animals, the images can be safely flipped horizontally to obtain a different posture of the same animal. It is an acceptable augmentation since animal can be found in left- or right-oriented condition. However, a vertical flipping would not be an acceptable augmentation in this case because animals are rarely found in an upside down condition under natural circumstances. Other standard augmentation techniques include affine and nonaffine transformations, perspective distortions, illumination variation, noise addition, and so on. While applying data augmentation techniques, we must take care to ensure that the augmented set of images could still be considered as acceptable input samples.

4) *Transfer learning*

The goal of generalization is to capture concepts that are generic enough so that they can model the entire input space, including the regions that are not represented within the training dataset. A human being that has not seen a tiger in his life can still recognize it as an animal because he has experience of other kinds of animals and is aware of the

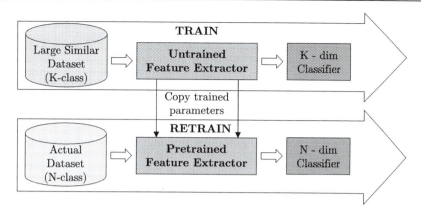

Figure 2.15: A graphical representation of transfer learning.

generic features that define an animal such as the presence of head, body, tail, legs, eyes, ears, and so on. This generalization of concepts allows humans to understand unseen samples with ease. The same can be achieved by transfer learning [41]. Transfer learning, as shown in Fig. 2.15, allows models to be trained in other relevant dataset to learn a generic set of features before being retrained in the problem dataset. It is useful when the problem dataset is smaller in size, but a larger dataset belonging to a similar is also available. For example, if a specific disease recognition task in a cytological dataset with only 100 samples needs to be carried out, then we can easily use concepts of transfer learning. Other large-scale publicly available cytological datasets (even for slightly different diseases) can be used to train randomly initialized neural networks. Though the features learnt by these networks correspond to different diseases, yet there will be some neurons that model generic shape, size, and colors of different cellular structures. These features can also be reused for the current problem. However, since this network is trained on a larger dataset, the features learnt are quite robust. Instead of training a randomly initialized network on the 100 problem images, this pretrained network can be retrained so that the weights are refined to adapt to the new problem domain. Transfer learning can also be implemented for semisupervised learning. In semisupervised learning a hidden representation $h = f(x)$ is learnt using an encoder network f. This is often achieved by an autoencoder, where the input is reconstructed as $x' = f'(h)$ by a decoder network f', which takes the output of the encoder h. The objective function minimizes the distance between input x and the reconstruction x' by a loss function such as a mean squared error $E_{MSE}(x, x')$. The trained encoder can be detached and prepended to a classifier layer and retrained to adapt new concepts. Since the input can be reconstructed from the hidden representation h by a decoder, h can be treated as a compressed representation of the input. This avoids spurious details from input space and focuses only on the essential components that contain the

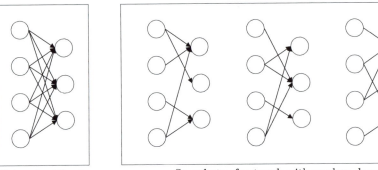

Network without   Snapshots of network with random dropout
Dropout   at different iterations

Figure 2.16: Dropout.

significant information about the properties of the sample. It is often seen that the samples
are much more well clustered in the hidden representation space as compared to the input
space. This allows networks to learn more generic features and prevent overfitting.

5) *Dropout*

Dropout is a concept for implementing the concept of "bagging in a single neural network" [42]. It is often seen that ensemble of multiple models are used for improving
the performance on a dataset. This is the concept of bagging. However, this seems im-
practical given that neural networks are computationally expensive models. Dropout is
implemented to mimic this method in fully connected hidden layers. The aim is to approximate the ensemble of all subnetworks of a neural network, which is obtained by
removing nonoutput connections of a underlying base network. Dropout performs this
approximation by randomly multiplying the output of a neuron by zero. This cutoff is carried out probabilistically. In practice the probability is kept at 0.5, that is, any nonoutput
edge has 50% probability of dropping off. As the process involves random drop of edges,
each time a sample is passed, it experiences a slightly different network configuration as
shown in Fig. 2.16. This allows each neuron to perform well under the absence of a fellow neuron, and hence more robust features are learnt. A network with lots of neurons can
model complex functions, but they are also prone to overfitting. However, due to dropout,
the training process never gets to enjoy the facility of all the neurons at once and hence
cannot overcomplicate the shape of the hyperplane. Thus dropout also serves as a regularizing agent.

6) *Parameter sharing*

One of the biggest contributions in the field of computer vision is the introduction of the
concepts of parameter sharing [43] in neural networks. This is one of the fundamental
concepts that led to the birth of convolutional neural networks. For computer vision tasks,

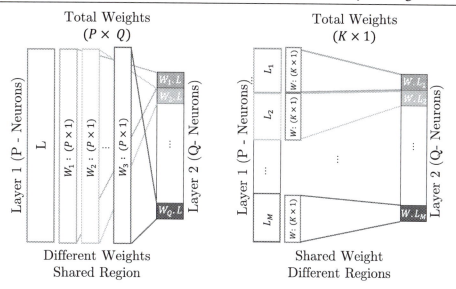

Figure 2.17: Parameter sharing: A fully connected network has different sets of weights working with all the input signals (left). In weight sharing the same set of weights is shared across different parths of the input signal (right).

neural networks take image samples as inputs. Now images are represented as a set of 2d arrays. For a grayscale image, one such 2d array of position-specific intensity values can suffice. For more higher-order color spaces such as RGB, RGBT, and so on, a 3d array is required, where the depth would be equal to the number of channels. To pass such an image into a neural network, it is possible to treat each pixel as an independent input signal. However, that would result in each pixel being associated with a different set of weights. However, in real world, images are filled with redundancies. Different regions of the image can have the same type of colors, gradients, or edges. Hence, without accounting for this redundancy, the learnt features tend to tightly adhere to the training samples rather than to learning basic features. With parameter sharing a smaller set of feature extracting neurons can be iteratively operated over different regions of the image providing information about the presence or absence of a feature in the corresponding regions. This type of nonredundant feature extraction is also seen in kernel-based approaches in classical image processing, which uses a family of filters such as Gabor, Gaussian, Sobel, Prewitt, Roberts, and so on. The benefit of feature extracting kernels is that kernels are composed of very low number of weights that can operate over large-sized images. Moreover, they are positionally invariant feature extractor and also much more generic as compared to fully connected neural layers. Fig. 2.17 demonstrates the idea of parameter sharing.

2.3 Convolutional neural networks

Standard multilayered perceptrons were built to process an array of signal and produce category specific spikes denoting the presence of a desired property. The networks are composed of multiple layers of fully connected neural layers. To pass the raw image through such a network, we need to treat each pixel of the image as a input signal, and a weight must be associated with it. So even a small image of 32×32 resolution will have 1024 input signals and 1024 weights for every hidden neuron in the first layer. This turns out to be extremely inefficient because the number of weights is simply too large to learn generic concepts. The common practice was representing the images as compressed low-dimensional vectors by using feature extraction techniques. This feature extraction can be carried out based on handcrafted rules set by domain experts or distribution-based automatic feature extraction like principal component analysis or singular value decomposition. However, methods like these fail to perform for more complicated datasets. This is either due to the fact that it is not possible to formulate a complicated set of rules by hand or the input distribution is too high-dimensional for automatic techniques to form clusters within permissible time. CNNs [44] address these issues to a great extent. The fundamental principle of CNNs are loosely based on the experiments of Hubel and Wiesel. They inserted a microelectrode into the primary visual cortex of a partially anesthetized cat to measure neurological responses as various images were shown to the cat. According to them, the visual cortex is organized in a hierarchical fashion. Whereas the neurons connected to the retina were primarily responsible for detecting basic shapes such as lines in various orientations, varying illuminations, and so on, the deeper layers of the cortex processed more complicated concepts such as geometric shapes, motions, and more complex visual features. CNNs draw inspiration from this model by rearranging standard neural network layers as low-level feature extracting modules that build on each other at every level and learn more complicated features along the depth. To understand CNNs, we need to look into several microconcepts such as kernel-based feature learning, weight sharing, and subsampling.

2.3.1 Feature extraction using convolutions

Convolutional neural networks are composed of layers composed of feature extracting elements. Building on the model of Hubel and Wiesel, the input layer needs standard edge and gradient detecting filters. The successive layers can then build more complex features by combining these simpler features. This is demonstrated in Fig. 2.18. In classic image processing, gradient and edge detection has been efficiently carried out by kernels such as Gabor, Sobel, and Prewitt. These kernels are made of tiny arrays of weights that can be aligned over a region of an image so that the corresponding weights and intensity values can be multiplied and summed to generate a response that signifies the presence of a gradient or edge.

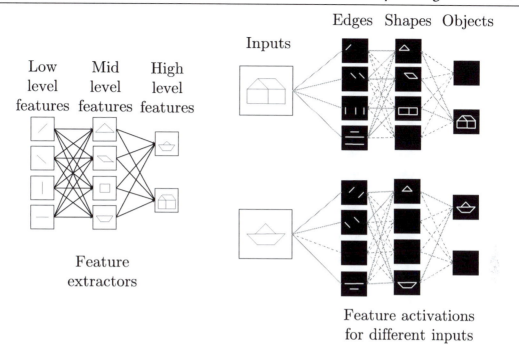

Figure 2.18: Learning strategy of CNNs.

Whereas in standard filters these weights are predefined, in CNN, these weights are trained by back-propagation. A convolution operation consists of sliding a kernel across the width and height of an array and computing the sum of products of the corresponding intensities and weights. Each kernel is also has a bias associated with it, which is added to the sum to form the response map. Every pixel of the response map is calculated by an operation of the sliding kernel at a specific location. Like standard neural networks, a nonlinear activation function plays a similar role in this case as well. The activation function maps each value of the response map to an activation map. The activation map is significant of the presence or absence of a feature across different parts of the image. Examples of activation maps are shown in Fig. 2.19. As the weights are shared across the span of the image, the number of parameters involved are significantly lesser, and due to the property of kernel-based operations, various low-level features like gradients, edges, spots, or even operations like blurring or sharpening can be carried out using convolutions. The convolution operation cannot only be carried out on the input image but also on an activation map and hence can be used to build subsequent layers. However, there are some things to be considered while building deeper layers such as field of view and sparsity of activations. These issues are addressed by subsampling.

Figure 2.19: Feature maps obtained from different layers of a CNN.

2.3.2 Subsampling

Convolution operations can operate both on input images and activation maps obtained from other convolution operations. However, as we build more layers, the aim is to learn more and more complex features. Although low-level features can be computed by exposing the kernel to small region of the image or, in other words, the kernels can have a small field of view to generate response, it is not the case for more complex features. For more complex features, the kernels must look over larger areas of the image or have a larger field of view. This can be done by increasing the kernel size, but that would also result in the increase in number of neurons. For example, $3 \times 3, 5 \times 5,$ and 7×7 kernels have 9, 25, and 49 neurons. To the computational overhead of linear operations, every neuron adds gradient computations and weight updates. So the other option would be keeping the size of the kernel small but reducing the size of the response maps so that the kernel operates over a larger field of view with respect to the original input. However, there is a concern that we might lose information reducing the size of the response maps. This is addressed in two ways. Firstly, the response maps by their nature have very low-level information like gradients, edges, and so on. So even if they are down-sampled, the information lost is pretty insignificant. Another factor is that at every layer, we use a multiple number of kernels. For K kernels, we have K different activation maps, and subsequent kernels convolve over all these maps at once. The standard practice is increasing the number of kernels as depth increases. This allows us to make up for some of

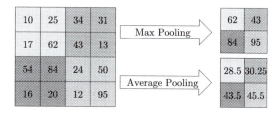

Figure 2.20: Max-pooling vs average pooling.

the lost representation space due to subsampling and also makes way for a larger number of complex features to built from smaller number of simpler features. This type of subsampling or down-sampling operations are carried out by pooling layers, which are layers consisting of sliding window operations. However, in contrast to convolution kernels, pooling kernels are windows that slide over regions of the input response map and the corresponding set of values is subsampled to a single pixel in the output response map (see Fig. 2.20). Depending on the nature of subsampling, pooling can be of two major types:

1) *Max-pooling*

   In max-pooling the maximum activation inside the pooling window is passed to the next layer, and all the other values are ignored. During back-propagation, the chain of partial derivatives break for nonmaximal activations inside a pooling window. Max-pooling is commonly used in intermediate layers, where activations are generally sparse in nature, and the information of the maximum activation dominates over that of the nonmaximal activations.

2) *Average pooling*

   Average pooling, as the name suggests, involves the passage of the average of the activations inside pooling window to the next layer. The chain of derivatives from the output response map splits equally along all the activation of the corresponding input response map. Average pooling is particularly useful when nonmaximal activations carry significant information. This is commonly used during converting spatial response maps to response vectors for fully connected layers, or in networks where spatially sensitive operations are carried out, such as localization or segmentation.

2.3.3 Effect of nonlinearity on activation maps

Like standard multilayered neural networks, CNNs also use nonlinear activation functions like the sigmoid or tanh. Whereas sigmoid and tanh functions are good activation functions for bounded activations, rectified linear units are often used activation maps inside CNNs. ReLUs convert all negative activations to zero but do not alter positive activations. This results in

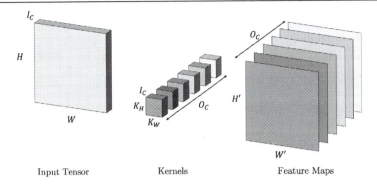

Figure 2.21: Hyperparameters of the convolution operation.

sparse activation maps, which reduces the number of nonzero multiplications and also complement quite well with operations like subsampling. However, softer activation functions like tanh and sigmoid are also useful in various cases where we require bounded outputs like in case of bounding box calculation, attention maps, and so on.

2.3.4 Layer design

While designing convolution layers some key factors must be kept in mind. Firstly, let us take a look at the hyperparameters that control these layers.

- Convolution: A convolution layer can be defined by several hyperparameters as shown in Fig. 2.21. It can be represented as a function $f_{\text{conv}}(C_{\text{in}}, C_{\text{out}}, K, S, P, D)$. The hyperparameters are defined as follows:
  - Input channels (C_{in}): This refers to the number of channels in the input map. The kernels that convolve over the input will have the same depth as C_{in}.
  - Output channels (C_{out}): This refers to the number of channels that will be produced by the layer. Basically, this is equal to the number of independent kernels that are being convoluted over the input.
  - Kernel Size (K): This is a tuple that refers to the height k_h and width k_w of the convolving kernels.
  - Stride (S): Stride is passed as a tuple (S_h, S_w) that signifies the number of pixels by which the kernels should slide along the height and width, respectively. With a stride of 1, the window slides one pixel at a time. This results in a response map, which is almost equal to the input map other than the lost boundary pixels. If the stride is set as 2, then the kernel slides with a step of 2 pixels, and the output response map has half the number of responses as before. Thus stride has a significant impact on the output map.

In several applications, strided convolutions are preferred over pooling operations because it provides us with a learnable variant of pooling that can be better for certain tasks like localization and segmentation.

- Padding (P): As the kernel has a bit of height and width, when it is convolved over the input, the output response maps are slightly smaller as the kernels cannot be centered over the boundary pixels because in that case parts of the kernel would be beyond the region of the image. Sometimes, it is useful to keep the output of the response map equal to that of the input map. For those cases, some dummy pixels are padded along the boundary to accommodate space for the kernel to align over the boundary pixels. Padding can be passed as a tuple as well, signifying the number of padding pixels along the height p_h and width p_h.

- Dilation (D): Dilation is way of increasing the field of view of kernel without increasing the number of parameters. Dilation is passed as a tuple (d_h, d_w) that defines the amounts of vertical and horizontal spacing between kernel weights, respectively. In this way a smaller-size kernel can align over a wider area of the input. This is often seen in applications like image segmentation.

The number of trainable weights for a layer is $C_{in} \times C_{out} \times k_h \times k_w$. In addition, there are C_{out} bias neurons b, one for each kernel that is added during the linear operation. The output for a kernel j and input x is given by

$$\text{out}_j = b_j + \sum_{i=0}^{C_{in}-1} w_{i,j} \times x_i. \tag{2.35}$$

The dimensions of output response map (H', W') for an input $(H \times W)$ are given by

$$H' = \left\lfloor \frac{H + 2 \times p_h - d_h \times (k_h - 1) - 1}{s_h} + 1 \right\rfloor \text{ and} \tag{2.36}$$

$$W' = \left\lfloor \frac{W + 2 \times p_w - d_w \times (k_w - 1) - 1}{s_w} + 1 \right\rfloor. \tag{2.37}$$

- Pooling: A pooling layer can also be defined by a set of hyperparameters as $f_{pool}(K, S)$.
  - Kernel Size (K): This is a tuple that refers to the height k_h and width k_w of the pooling window.
  - Stride (S): Stride is passed as tuple (S_h, S_w) that signifies the number of pixels by which the pooling should slide along the height and width, respectively. It works as in the case of convolutions.

A standard practice for intermediate layers is using a kernel size and stride of 2 to halve the size of the response map. Sometimes, for average pooling, a spatial response map of

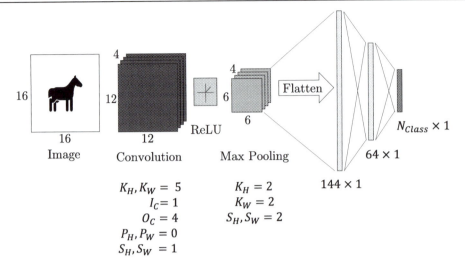

Figure 2.22: A sample CNN.

dimensions $H \times W$ is pooled with a window of the same dimensions. In this case the output would be a linear vector. This is useful for converting spatial response maps to vectors for passing into classifier layers, which are simple fully connected layers.

A sample CNN is shown in Fig. 2.22 for demonstration purposes.

Bonus tips

Convolution layers are often followed by batch-normalization layers [45]. Batch normalization utilizes the concept of minibatch learning protocol to normalize the response maps across the batch dimension. This allows a regularizing effect as features need to produce informative content for not one but a batch of images.

Activation functions are mandatory after convolutional layers to introduce nonlinearity into the system. ReLU [30,31] is the most commonly used activation, but other functions like sigmoid or tanh activations also find their use for applications, such as visual attention, localization, and segmentation.

When building deep networks, one of the easiest ways to facilitate gradient propagation in very deep networks is providing a skip connection or shortcut connection across every 2 or 3 convolutional layers. If a set of convolution functions is represented as $f(x)$, then the output signal along with a skip connection is given by $y = f(x) + x$. During back-propagation, the gradient across the shortcut connection would be unity and hence would facilitate fast gradient propagation across large depths. This was introduced in the residual network [46], which will be discussed later.

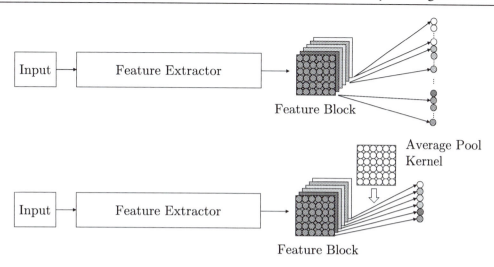

Figure 2.23: Average pooling versus tensor flattening for conversion of spatial representation to feature embeddings.

Sometimes features are not captured by a kernel of single width and height. Parallel branches computing feature maps with differently sized kernels can later be concatenated to create multiscale feature maps [47].

2.3.5 Output layer

Convolutional layers are good for feature extraction from images as they deal with the spatial redundancy by weight sharing. As we go deeper down the network, the features become more exclusive and informative, and redundancy is reduced. This is primarily due to repeated cascaded convolutions and information compression by subsampling layers. As redundancy is reduced, we end up with a compressed feature representation about the content of the image. Now output layers deal with mapping this feature to necessary output categories. This mapping function does not require any weight sharing anymore because the entire feature vector is needed to make informative decision. The standard practice is converting the learned features from the convolutional feature extractors to a vector that works as a image descriptor. This conversion can be done in two ways, which are shown in Fig. 2.23. One way is to simply reshape all the activations of the last layer of the feature extractor into a one-dimensional tensor [44,48]. The second method is using a full-scale average pooling. For an activation map of resolution $h \times w$, an average pool with a kernel of the same resolution $h \times w$ will reduce the map to a scalar value signifying the gross activation [46,47]. This way the last layer can be mapped to a feature vector. This vector is then connected to the output classifier. The

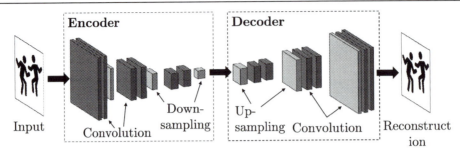

Encoder

Decoder

Input

Convolution

Down-sampling

Up-sampling

Convolution

Reconstruction

Figure 2.24: Autoencoders.

classifier is a standard multilayer consisting of optional hidden layers and an output layer with the requisite number of output neurons that map from the feature descriptor to the output space.

2.4 Encoder–decoder architecture

Multilayer perceptrons were primarily built to perform supervised learning. The back-propagation algorithm that drives the weight updating in the neural network requires an objective function that reduces the difference between the observed output and a desired output. In most general cases the desired output is derived from a ground truth that drives the training procedure. However, in the late 1980s the introduction of autoassociative networks [49] provided a new kind of architecture called autoencoders. The principle behind autoencoders is encoding raw inputs into a latent representation. A decoder network attempts to reconstruct the input from the encoded representation. This is shown in Fig. 2.24. The minimization of a loss function based on the difference of the input and the reconstructed output ensures minimum loss of information in the intermediate representation. This hidden representation is a compressed form of the actual input. This kind of encoder–decoder architectures were built to function as one of the first neural networks capable of automatic feature extraction; however, the model found other applications in the supervised learning domain as well.

One of the most straightforward applications is unsupervised feature extraction. The compressed representation can serve as a good feature set because it encodes most of the information of the input space but reduces redundancy. Different samples that are cluttered in the input space tend to form nice separate clusters in the latent representation space. This feature set can be further used for other machine learning tasks. After a encoder–decoder network is trained, the decoder can be clipped off, and the encoder can be attached to a classifier to perform transfer learning tasks.

The encoder–decoder architecture can also be used for other spatially sensitive supervised problems by tweaking the loss function. Instead of reducing a loss between the actual input and reconstructed input, a pixel-level or region-level loss function can also be used to perform several complicated tasks, such as segmentation [19,50,51] or localization [52].

2.4.1 Unsupervised learning in CNNs

Unsupervised learning is not only limited to multilayered perceptrons. It is also applicable to CNNs. In autoencoders the encoder is the feature extractor, whereas the decoders have some generative properties that can produce complicated high-resolution activation maps. In autoencoders, this generative property is exploited to reconstruct the input itself to ensure that the most distinguishing features of the image are not lost within the latent representation. Whereas encoders in CNNs can be built in standard way as a sequence of convolution and pooling operations, the decoder is a bit tricky. The resolution of the image progressively decreases along the depth of the encoder. The decoder must be able to increase the resolution progressively. This upscaling of activation maps can be done in three ways.

1) *Interpolation:*
   The easiest way to upsample an activation map is to simply do it by bilinear or nearest-neighbor interpolation. This kind of processes is very lightweight, less prone to cause any irregularities, but produces softer upscaled maps. The blurred activations can be sharpened by some convolution layers following the upsample layer.
2) *Transposed convolution:*
   Transposed convolution, also known as convolution with fractional strides, has been introduced to reverse the effects of a traditional convolution operation [53]. It is often referred to as deconvolution. However, deconvolution, as defined in signal processing, is different from transposed convolution in terms of the basic formulation, although they effectively address the same problem. In a convolution operation, there is a change in size of the input based on the amount of padding and stride of the kernels. A stride of 2 will create half the number of activations as that of a stride of 1. For a transposed convolution to work, padding and stride should be controlled in a way that the size change is reversed. This is achieved by dilating the input space. Note that unlike atrous convolutions, where the kernels were dilated, here the input spaces are dilated.
3) *Unpooling:*
   Another approach to reduce the size of the activations is through pooling layers. A 2×2 pooling layer with a stride of two reduces the height and width of the image by a factor of 2. In such a pooling layer, a 2×2 neighborhood of pixel is compressed to a single pixel. Different types of pooling performs the compression in different ways.

Image   Segmentation   Localization

Figure 2.25: Image segmentation and localization.

Max-pooling considers the maximum activation value among 4 pixels, whereas average pooling takes an average of the same. A corresponding unpooling layer decompresses a single pixel to a neighborhood of 2×2 pixels to double the height and width of the image [54].

2.4.2 Image-to-image translation

These techniques can also be used for supervised learning tasks. Image-to-image translation models can create an image output, which is a transformed variant of the actual image. They are applied, for example, to segmentation [51], image restoration [55], image denoising [56], and image colorization [57]. The loss function is computed at a pixel level that aims to reduce the difference between the generated tensor and a desired tensor. The desired tensor cannot only be other images as in cases of image restoration or image colorization but also pixel-level class indicators as in case of segmentation.

2.4.3 Localization

Encoder–decoder networks have also found their use in localization where multiresolution outputs signifying the presence and shape of bounding boxes can also be learnt [52]. Each region or pixel in this can contain the information about the presence of a bounding box centroid, shape of a bounding box, and confidence scores. Fig. 2.25 shows desired outputs for image segmentation and localization tasks.

2.4.4 Multiscale feature propagation

As the encoders reduce the resolution of the image, decoding straightaway from the compressed representation can result in blurry reconstructions for supervised tasks. As shown

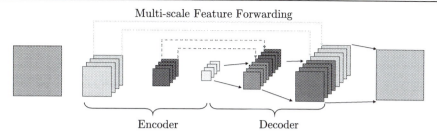

Figure 2.26: Skip connections for multiscale feature propagation.

in Fig. 2.26, this can be sorted out by passing skipping branches from features of multiple scales in the encoder to relevant layers of decoder to sharpen the activation maps in each layer [51].

References

[1] Warren S. McCulloch, Walter Pitts, A logical calculus of the ideas immanent in nervous activity, The Bulletin of Mathematical Biophysics 5 (4) (1943) 115–133.

[2] D.O. Hebb, The organization of behaviour: a neuropsychological study, 1949.

[3] Frank Rosenblatt, The perceptron: a probabilistic model for information storage and organization in the brain, Psychological Review 65 (6) (1958) 386.

[4] Bernard Widrow, et al., Adaptive "adaline" neuron using chemical "memistors", 1960.

[5] Seymour Papert, Linearly unrecognizable patterns, Mathematical Aspects of Computer Science 19 (1967) 176.

[6] Kunihiko Fukushima, Sei Miyake, Neocognitron: a self-organizing neural network model for a mechanism of visual pattern recognition, in: Competition and Cooperation in Neural Nets, Springer, 1982, pp. 267–285.

[7] Kunihiko Fukushima, Neocognitron: a hierarchical neural network capable of visual pattern recognition, Neural Networks 1 (2) (1988) 119–130.

[8] David H. Hubel, Torsten N. Wiesel, Receptive fields, binocular interaction and functional architecture in the cat's visual cortex, The Journal of Physiology 160 (1) (1962) 106–154.

[9] David E. Rumelhart, Geoffrey E. Hinton, Ronald J. Williams, Learning representations by back-propagating errors, Nature 323 (6088) (1986) 533–536.

[10] Yoshua Bengio, Patrice Simard, Paolo Frasconi, Learning long-term dependencies with gradient descent is difficult, IEEE Transactions on Neural Networks 5 (2) (1994) 157–166.

[11] David H. Ackley, Geoffrey E. Hinton, Terrence J. Sejnowski, A learning algorithm for Boltzmann machines, Cognitive Science 9 (1) (1985) 147–169.

[12] Geoffrey E. Hinton, Simon Osindero, Yee-Whye Teh, A fast learning algorithm for deep belief nets, Neural Computation 18 (7) (2006) 1527–1554.

[13] KC Santosh, Sameer K. Antani, Automated chest X-ray screening: can lung region symmetry help detect pulmonary abnormalities?, IEEE Transactions on Medical Imaging 37 (5) (2018) 1168–1177, https://doi.org/10.1109/TMI.2017.2775636.

[14] KC Santosh, Szilárd Vajda, Sameer K. Antani, George R. Thoma, Edge map analysis in chest X-rays for automatic pulmonary abnormality screening, International Journal of Computer Assisted Radiology and Surgery 11 (9) (2016) 1637–1646, https://doi.org/10.1007/s11548-016-1359-6.

[15] Szilárd Vajda, Alexandros Karargyris, Stefan Jäger, KC Santosh, Sema Candemir, Zhiyun Xue, Sameer K. Antani, George R. Thoma, Feature selection for automatic tuberculosis screening in frontal chest radiographs, Journal of Medical Systems 42 (8) (2018) 146, https://doi.org/10.1007/s10916-018-0991-9.

[16] Dipayan Das, KC Santosh, Umapada Pal, Truncated inception net: Covid-19 outbreak screening using chest X-rays, Physical Engineering Sciences in Medicine 8 (2020) 1–11, https://doi.org/10.1007/s13246-020-00888-x.

[17] Alexandros Karargyris, Jenifer Siegelman, Dimitris Tzortzis, Stefan Jaeger, Sema Candemir, Zhiyun Xue, KC Santosh, Szilárd Vajda, Sameer K. Antani, Les R. Folio, George R. Thoma, Combination of texture and shape features to detect pulmonary abnormalities in digital chest X-rays, International Journal of Computer Assisted Radiology and Surgery 11 (1) (2016) 99–106, https://doi.org/10.1007/s11548-015-1242-x.

[18] KC Santosh, Laurent Wendling, Sameer K. Antani, George R. Thoma, Overlaid arrow detection for labeling regions of interest in biomedical images, IEEE Intelligent Systems 31 (3) (2016) 66–75, https://doi.org/10.1109/MIS.2016.24.

[19] Swarnendu Ghosh, Anisha Pal, Shourya Jaiswal, KC Santosh, Nibaran Das, Mita Nasipuri, SegFast-V2: semantic image segmentation with less parameters in deep learning for autonomous driving, International Journal of Machine Learning and Cybernetics 10 (11) (2019) 3145–3154.

[20] KC Santosh, Laurent Wendling, Angular relational signature-based chest radiograph image view classification, Medical & Biological Engineering & Computing 56 (8) (2018) 1447–1458, https://doi.org/10.1007/s11517-018-1786-3.

[21] Sourodip Ghosh, Ahana Bandyopadhyay, Shreya Sahay, Richik Ghosh, Ishita Kundu, KC Santosh, Colorectal histology tumor detection using ensemble deep neural network, in: Engineering Applications of Artificial Intelligence, 2021.

[22] KC Santosh, Amit Joshi, Covid-19: Prediction, Decision-Making, and Its Impacts, Lecture Notes on Data Engineering and Communications Technologies, 2020.

[23] Amit Joshi, Nilanjan Dey, KC Santosh, Intelligent Systems and Methods to Combat Covid-19, Springer Briefs in Computational Intelligence, 2020.

[24] KC Santosh, AI-driven tools for coronavirus outbreak: need of active learning and cross-population train/test models on multitudinal/multimodal data, Journal of Medical Systems 44 (5) (2020) 93, https://doi.org/10.1007/s10916-020-01562-1.

[25] KC Santosh, COVID-19 prediction models and unexploited data, Journal of Medical Systems 44 (9) (2020) 170, https://doi.org/10.1007/s10916-020-01645-z.

[26] H. Mukherjee, S. Ghosh, A. Dhar, S.M. Obaidullah, KC Santosh, K. Roy, Deep neural network to detect COVID-19: one architecture for both CT scans and chest X-rays, Applied Intelligence 51 (2021) 2777–2789, https://doi.org/10.1007/s10489-020-01943-6.

[27] H. Mukherjee, A. Dhar, S.M. Obaidullah, KC Santosh, K. Roy, Shallow convolutional neural network for Covid-19 outbreak screening using chest X-rays, in: Cognitive Computation, 2021, https://doi.org/10.1007/s12559-020-09775-9.

[28] KC Santosh, Sourodip Ghosh, Covid-19 imaging tools: how big data is big?, Journal of Medical Systems 45 (7) (2021) 71, https://doi.org/10.1007/s10916-021-01747-2.

[29] KC Santosh, S. Antani, D.S. Guru, N. Dey, Medical Imaging: Artificial Intelligence, Image Recognition, and Machine Learning Techniques, 1st ed., MCRC Press, 2019.

[30] Vinod Nair, Geoffrey E. Hinton, Rectified linear units improve restricted Boltzmann machines, in: ICML, 2010.

[31] Xavier Glorot, Antoine Bordes, Yoshua Bengio, Deep sparse rectifier neural networks, in: Proceedings of the Fourteenth International Conference on Artificial Intelligence and Statistics, 2011, pp. 315–323.

[32] Herbert Robbins, Sutton Monro, A stochastic approximation method, The Annals of Mathematical Statistics (1951) 400–407.

[33] Boris T. Polyak, Some methods of speeding up the convergence of iteration methods, USSR Computational Mathematics and Mathematical Physics 4 (5) (1964) 1–17.

[34] Fangyu Zou, Li Shen, Zequn Jie, Weizhong Zhang, Wei Liu, A sufficient condition for convergences of Adam and RMSProp, in: Proceedings of the IEEE Conference on Computer Vision and Pattern Recognition, 2019, pp. 11127–11135.

[35] Diederik P. Kingma, Jimmy Ba, Adam: a method for stochastic optimization, in: Proceedings of the 3rd International Conference on Learning Representations (ICLR), 2014.

[36] Cullen Schaffer, Overfitting avoidance as bias, Machine Learning 10 (2) (1993) 153–178.

[37] Warren S. Sarle, Stopped training and other remedies for overfitting, Computing Science and Statistics (1996) 352–360.

[38] Anders Krogh, John A. Hertz, A simple weight decay can improve generalization, in: Advances in Neural Information Processing Systems, 1992, pp. 950–957.

[39] Martin A. Tanner, Wing Hung Wong, The calculation of posterior distributions by data augmentation, Journal of the American Statistical Association 82 (398) (1987) 528–540.

[40] David A. Van Dyk, Xiao-Li Meng, The art of data augmentation, Journal of Computational and Graphical Statistics 10 (1) (2001) 1–50.

[41] Sinno Jialin Pan, Qiang Yang, A survey on transfer learning, IEEE Transactions on Knowledge and Data Engineering 22 (10) (2009) 1345–1359.

[42] Nitish Srivastava, Geoffrey Hinton, Alex Krizhevsky, Ilya Sutskever, Ruslan Salakhutdinov, Dropout: a simple way to prevent neural networks from overfitting, Journal of Machine Learning Research 15 (1) (2014) 1929–1958.

[43] Steven J. Nowlan, Geoffrey E. Hinton, Simplifying neural networks by soft weight-sharing, Neural Computation 4 (4) (1992) 473–493.

[44] Yann LeCun, Léon Bottou, Yoshua Bengio, Patrick Haffner, Gradient-based learning applied to document recognition, Proceedings of the IEEE 86 (11) (1998) 2278–2324.

[45] Sergey Ioffe, Christian Szegedy, Batch normalization: accelerating deep network training by reducing internal covariate shift, preprint, arXiv:1502.03167, 2015.

[46] Kaiming He, Xiangyu Zhang, Shaoqing Ren, Jian Sun, Deep residual learning for image recognition, in: Proceedings of the IEEE Conference on Computer Vision and Pattern Recognition, 2016, pp. 770–778.

[47] Christian Szegedy, Wei Liu, Yangqing Jia, Pierre Sermanet, Scott Reed, Dragomir Anguelov, Dumitru Erhan, Vincent Vanhoucke, Andrew Rabinovich, Going deeper with convolutions, in: Proceedings of the IEEE Conference on Computer Vision and Pattern Recognition, 2015, pp. 1–9.

[48] Alex Krizhevsky, Ilya Sutskever, Geoffrey E. Hinton, ImageNet classification with deep convolutional neural networks, in: Advances in Neural Information Processing Systems, 2012, pp. 1097–1105.

[49] Mark A. Kramer, Autoassociative neural networks, Computers & Chemical Engineering 16 (4) (1992) 313–328.

[50] Vijay Badrinarayanan, Alex Kendall, Roberto Cipolla Segnet, A deep convolutional encoder–decoder architecture for image segmentation, IEEE Transactions on Pattern Analysis and Machine Intelligence 39 (12) (2017) 2481–2495.

[51] Olaf Ronneberger, Philipp Fischer, Thomas Brox U-net, Convolutional networks for biomedical image segmentation, in: International Conference on Medical Image Computing and Computer-Assisted Intervention, Springer, 2015, pp. 234–241.

[52] Joseph Redmon, Ali Farhadi, Yolov3: an incremental improvement, preprint, arXiv:1804.02767, 2018.

[53] Matthew D. Zeiler, Dilip Krishnan, Graham W. Taylor, Rob Fergus, Deconvolutional networks, in: 2010 IEEE Computer Society Conference on Computer Vision and Pattern Recognition, IEEE, 2010, pp. 2528–2535.

[54] Hyeonwoo Noh, Seunghoon Hong, Bohyung Han, Learning deconvolution network for semantic segmentation, in: Proceedings of the IEEE International Conference on Computer Vision, 2015, pp. 1520–1528.

[55] Xiaojiao Mao, Chunhua Shen, Yu-Bin Yang, Image restoration using very deep convolutional encoder–decoder networks with symmetric skip connections, in: Advances in Neural Information Processing Systems, 2016, pp. 2802–2810.

[56] Pascal Vincent, Hugo Larochelle, Isabelle Lajoie, Yoshua Bengio, Pierre-Antoine Manzagol, Léon Bottou, Stacked denoising autoencoders: learning useful representations in a deep network with a local denoising criterion, Journal of Machine Learning Research 11 (12) (2010).

[57] Richard Zhang, Phillip Isola, Alexei A. Efros, Colorful image colorization, in: European Conference on Computer Vision, Springer, 2016, pp. 649–666.

CHAPTER 3

Deep learning models

3.1 Deep learning models

While building deep learning models, there are several factors that must be taken into account. The three factors that are essential to optimize the network are the design of the objective function, the network architecture, and the learning strategy. Each of these three factors is closely interconnected in a way that must be tuned properly according to the problem domain.

3.1.1 Learning different objectives

Deep learning models in general are trained on the basis of an objective function, but the way in which the objective function is designed reveals a lot about the purpose of the model. With this, for more understanding, in what follows, we discuss learning models with and without labels, reward-based models, and multiobjective optimization.

1) *Learning with labels:*

   Standard supervised models require a predefined desired output. Deep learning models take this supervision into account by designing the loss function as the difference between the predicted output and a representation of the desired output. The two basic categories of supervised learning techniques, classification and regression, are both easily interpreted by deep neural networks [1]. Classification problems generally have a sample associated with one or more classes from a predefined set of categories. The output layer of the network has same number of neurons as the total number of classes. The objective function generally computes a loss function that signifies the difference between the output vector and a probability distribution representing the desired class values. For single-class problems, this probability distribution would be a one-hot vector [2]. In cases like these, negative log likelihood is an ideal option for a loss function as it is extremely fast and the number of computations is independent of the number of classes. For multi-label problems where a sample can belong to more than one class, things can get tricky. One option can be representing the output as a marginal distribution, and hence every output neuron follows a binomial distribution. The loss function can be represented as the sum over several binary cross entropy functions [3]. Another approach is modeling the output as a multinomial distribution, where each class has a certain probability of occurrence. A more generic categorical cross entropy function is more appropriate for cases like these. Many other tasks can also be reduced to classification problems. For example, image segmentation can be treated as a pixel-level classification problem, where an output vector generates a probability distribution for each pixel of the image [4]. Similarly, a sequence generation problem can be treated as a sequence of classifications in a vocabulary space. Other examples of supervised learning are in the form of regression problems. Deep learning networks can also be used to generated real-valued outputs. In cases like this the output tensor is of the same shape as a desired tensor, and a mean squared error loss between the two is used for back-propagation. This has several applications in case of generative tasks such as sample reconstruction or score predictions. Another variant of regression is for density estimation problem where a KL divergence loss function is used.

2) *Learning without labels:*
   One of the most common implementations of unsupervised learning algorithms can be seen in case of autoencoders [5]. Autoencoders are networks designed to map the samples from an input space to a fixed-dimensional feature space, from which the input is reconstructed. The reconstruction loss can be a simple mean squared error of the predicted and actual inputs. No other ground truth is necessary for computing the feature space. Naturally, the compressed feature space must be quite successful in encoding the information of the input space if the reconstruction is almost equal to the input. This kind of networks has several applications such as unsupervised clustering, feature extraction, or even in transfer learning problems.

3) *Reward-based models:*
   Rewards are numerical values denoting the success or failure of an operation. The goal of reward-based models is computing an optimal policy gradient that updates the decision-making process based on the probability of gaining a reward. The most common application for such models is in reinforcement learning [6].

4) *Multiobjective optimization:*
   Deep learning networks need not be limited to a single objective function. Loss values from multiple objective functions can be combined in various ways to learn several objectives at the same time [7]. An example of such an application is the joint optimization in a joint reduction of classification loss along with parameter norm penalty for regularization.

3.1.2 Network structure for CNNs

In early days, deep learning networks started as simple cascaded layers of neurons. Later, complex networks started to rise. We discuss some of the notable design philosophies of CNNs. These are graphically shown in Fig. 3.1.

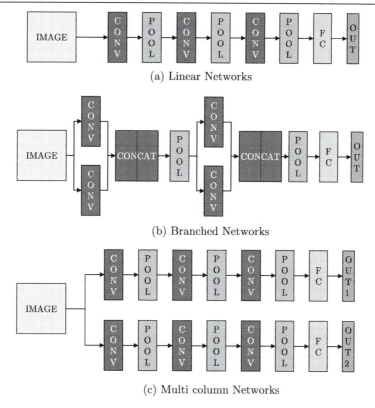

(a) Linear Networks

(b) Branched Networks

(c) Multi column Networks

Figure 3.1: Different design philosophies of CNNs.

1) *Linear networks:*

The most basic models of convolutional neural networks start with low number of kernels producing large activation maps in the earlier layers. As the depth increases, the size of the activation maps gets reduced. To compensate for the increasing in the number of represented concepts, the number of kernels is increased. This creates a pyramid-like structure of feature maps starting with wide and slimmer activation maps and ending with narrower yet deeper blocks. The standard protocol is to double the number of features every time the height and width are halved due to subsampling. This practice is still followed as one of the thumb rules of designing CNNs [1,2,8].

2) *Branched networks:*

With the progress of research in the field of deep learning, the networks began to exhibit various interesting topologies. One of the most common developments was the use of parallel branches consisting of different types of feature extracting elements. The variety existed in the form of different types of kernels, squeeze and excitation blocks, skip connections, shake-drop branches, and so on. Each of these modules addresses several factors

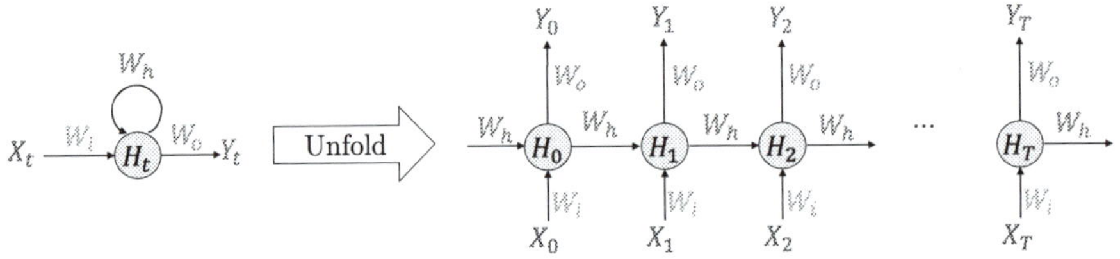

Figure 3.2: Unfolding RNNs.

such as increasing field of view, applying attention to learned features, easier gradient flow, and more [9–11].

3) *Multicolumn networks:*

Multicolumn networks can be considered as a set of similar or different networks that parallely operates on multiple copies of the input or some variations of the same. Multi-column networks [12–16] can also be used for operating on separate regions of the image or for attending different objectives. Multicolumn networks are incredibly popular on datasets with deformable components in image samples or complex scenes that require fine-grained parsing.

3.1.3 Types of models based on learning strategies

As network models can be highly customized based on the objective function, the learning strategy also plays a significant role.

1) *Back-propagation against well-defined loss functions:*

This is the most straightforward implementation where a loss function signifies the difference between the observed and desired outputs. The back-propagation algorithm simply passes the gradient corresponding to the loss function down the depth of the network.

2) *Back-propagation across time:*

This kind of learning phenomena is commonly seen in recurrent neural networks. Due the feedback loop, a simple recurrent neural network can be unfurled to create a long chain of computations. Each link in this chain denotes a time-stamp after which a branch from the output is fed back to the beginning of the network. As it is unfurled, the backward flow of gradients is a flow across the various time-stamps as shown in Fig. 3.2. This has significant applications in video analysis and text processing.

3) *Reinforcement learning:*

Reinforcement learning revolves around a reward-based optimization paradigm. Intelligent agents can learn to take a series of decisions in an environment to maximize a reward. Unlike supervised learning, there are no labels provided. This type of learning focuses on finding a balance between exploration (unknown effects of actions) and exploitation (known effects of actions).

4) *Adversarial learning:*

Adversarial learning strategies focus on the concept training a network to be robust against some kind of corruption or forgery. It has significant applications in securing neural networks and generative models. Adversarial attacks can be performed by trained networks to make other machine learning model perform poorly. This type of learning is often used in applications such avoiding spam detections. From another perspective, by training networks to withstand such adversarial attacks, the quality of features learnt can improve. This is also used in generative networks where deep neural networks are used to approximate a sample space. The sample generated by this network must be able to beat an adversarial agent that distinguishes fake samples from real samples.

5) *Transfer learning:*

Deep learning algorithms perform best when there is a lot of well-curated data samples, but it is not always feasible to arrange for collection and annotation of large number of samples for every new problem domain. Transfer learning strategies can aid in this matter to a great extent. Transfer learning can occur in two different ways. One way is to first train a network on a larger dataset that contains similar samples as the smaller problem dataset and then to retrain the learned weights to fit the necessary output distribution. In this way the features learned are much more generalized and robust as compared to a network that is trained only on the small dataset. Another implementation of transfer learning is transfer features learnt from a different objective to a new objective function. For example, to learn generalized features for a classification task, we might train an autoencoder to cluster the sample space and create an informative hidden representation with much less redundancy and noise. The features from the end of the encoder part of this autoencoder can be connected to a classifier that maps it to the output layer. Then if that network is retrained on the labels defined in the problem, then a much more generalized fit can be obtained.

3.2 Elements in deep learning pipeline

The process of building deep learning-based applications requires several key decisions regarding data processing, model selection, training and validation, and so on.

3.2.1 Data preprocessing

The quality and quantity of well-annotated data are a key for the success of deep learning applications. In the field of computer vision, data samples are mostly available in the format of images or videos. Before feeding into deep neural networks, images must be preprocessed to some extent. Some of the most common preprocessings are summarized as follows.

1) *Resizing the input to a specific resolution:*
   One of the most common preprocessings is reshaping the image to a predefined resolution [17]. Most CNNs impose some constraints regarding the resolution of the input image, which, if not maintained, might prevent the network from producing a desirable output.

2) *Whitening transform:*
   It is a method of normalizing an image with respect to the data distribution such that the covariance matrix is an identity matrix. This allows the network to avoid too small or overblown gradients, which in turn aid in gradient propagation.

3) *Augmentation:*
   Data augmentation is another common approach to improve performance of deep neural networks [18]. Depending on the type of data, various augmentation techniques can be used to increase the size of the dataset. Some commonly used augmentation techniques are affine or nonaffine transformations like translation, rotation, skewing, scaling, flipping, warping, perspective distortion, and so on. To induce noise robustness, inputs can sometimes also be accompanied by noise.

3.2.2 Model selection

Once we have a fixed the problem domain and have access to a reasonable amount of data samples, the next step would be to decide on the type of model to be used. While selecting a model or designing one from scratch, there are three key factors that should be kept in mind. We summarize them as follows.

1) *Input type:*
   Input samples define the structure of the earlier part of the network. A vector input can be passed as a single-dimensional tensor, whereas a simple grayscale image requires only a single-channel 2d tensor as input. Colored images, generally represented in the RGB format, are passed as a 3d tensor with 3 channels. Images can also be represented in other color spaces or even in different spectra. In such cases, we might use an input with even higher number of channels or even a series of feature extraction layers working individually on separate channels.

2) *Objective function:*
   The second aspect of designing a model is determining the objective function. The objective function determines the shape of the output tensor. For example, a classification problem will have a vector output composed of logits corresponding to each class, whereas for

a segmentation problem, the output would be a 3d tensor having a width and height that is the same as the original image, and the depth assigns a class distribution for each pixel. These factors have an obvious impact on model design or selection. The other most obvious factor that comes into play in this regard is the primary goal of the problem itself. There is a variety of objective functions curated to attend different problem scenarios such as mean squared errors, cross entropy, negative log likelihood, soft margin loss, dice loss, and so on. Each of these loss functions addresses various problem domains such as regression, classification, segmentation, and so on. However, loss functions are not limited by the direct objectives. It can further be enhanced to take other factors into account such as regularization, multiobjective learning, adversarial learning, and gradient boosting.

3) *Data complexity:*

While the previous two factors determine the earlier and latter layers of the network, the middle portion is responsible for representing the actual concepts that encompass the data. This is the bulk of the network, and this determines how well the network maps from the input to the output. Various factors should be considered while designing a deep neural network. The neurons in a network can be increased in two directions, width and depth. In simpler terms, as the neurons or kernels are arranged as a cascade of several layers, we can increase the number of neurons or kernels in each layer that is the width of each layer or increase the number of layers in the network that is the depth of the network. Although there is no hard and fast rule to determine the exact number of neurons and layers necessary for optimal performance, some common thumb rules can be followed. The overall number of necessary neurons and the complexity of the topology of network are directly proportional to the complexity of the data. For example, classifying black and white images of handwritten digits [19] is a much simpler task than classifying colored images [20] such as of animals because the former has a much lower degree of freedom in the input space. The depth in the network is often responsible for learning complex features made from the combination of simpler low-level features. Hence if the data requires lots of complex high-level features for proper representation, then a deeper network is advised. However, if the data require a more number of features in the same level of complexity, then the number kernels or neurons can be increased in a specific layer, or the width of network can be increased. Another important aspect associated with the depth in case of convolutional neural network is the scale of the features extracted. Deeper layers will have kernels that process features over a larger field of view of the image. This is another aspect, where we can determine how much of the global information we allow to affect the output. This is a particularly important decision for segmentation problems, as deeper networks obtain more complex features, but the spatial representation loses sharpness as the feature maps gets reduced in size. In cases like this, where both depth and sharpness are necessary, it is advisable to use features drawn from different levels of the network to build the output.

3.2.3 Model validation and hyperparameter tuning

As the model is trained on a set of training data, it is expected to perform well on samples from that set. However, for unseen samples, the network may or may not perform at the same level. This is controlled by the amount of regularization in the network that prevents it from overfitting. To make sure that the model is capable of performing on unseen samples, a validation set may be used, which consists of some samples that the network has not seen during the weight updation process. During validation, a suitable performance metric may be chosen to measure the capability of the network. Although the objective function is a good measure of the performance, however, most of the time the goal of the network is measured using some other metrics. For example, in a classification problem a common performance measure is the accuracy defined as

$$\text{Accuracy} = \frac{\text{No. of correctly classified samples}}{\text{Total no. of samples}}. \tag{3.1}$$

The accuracy metric is significant for the global performance, but it does not reveal how the network performs for individual classes. Precision, Recall, and F-measures are more sensitive metrics in this sense. These metrics are designed specifically for binary class problems; however, they can be used for multiclass problems by generating a corresponding metric for each class separately. These metrics are based on performance of the network in each class in a one-vs-all fashion. For each class c, this may be described in 4 ways:

- True Positive (TP): A true positive is when a sample is correctly classified as belonging to class c.
- False Positive (FP): A false positive is when a sample is incorrectly classified as belonging to class c.
- True Negative (TN): A true negative is when a sample is correctly classified as not belonging to class c.
- False Negative (FN): A false negative is when a sample is incorrectly classified as not belonging to class c.

Precision, Recall, and F-measures are calculated as

$$\text{Precision (P)} = \frac{\text{TP}}{\text{TP} + \text{FP}}, \tag{3.2}$$

$$\text{Recall (R)} = \frac{\text{TP}}{\text{TP} + \text{FN}}, \tag{3.3}$$

$$\text{F-measure} = \frac{2PR}{P + R}. \tag{3.4}$$

Though these measures are class-specific measures, they can be averaged over all classes to signify an overall performance. Whereas Precision defines the ratio of how accurately the network can claim a sample as positive, Recall defines how many of the total positive samples can the network recognize. Depending on the problem scenario, more importance may be given to either Precision or Recall. For example, when detecting the presence of a disease, Recall proves to be a more important metric as the a false negative is much more harmful for the patient than a false positive as a sick patient may be classified as disease free. However, for a problem like spam detection, a false positive might flag an important mail as spam. So Precision is a more important metric in this case. For binary class problems, a Precision–Recall curve may be used to demonstrate the performance of the network by manipulating various threshold levels.

These are various types of performance metrics. They mostly vary depending on the type of the problem. Other problems like segmentation use mean intersection of unions as a measure of the similarity between observed and actual segments. Sequential problems like caption generation use measures like perplexity or BERT scores.

These performance metrics can be used to validate a model to measure its robustness against unseen data. Whereas the weights are the primary parameters of the network and are updated by the means of the back-propagation algorithm, there are several other hyperparameters that control the overall performance on the data space. As described earlier in this section, there are several decisions involved while building the deep learning pipeline, such as

- Type of data preprocessing;
- The various types of layers in the network;
- The number of neurons in each layer;
- The number of epochs;
- Regularization strategy; and
- Learning rate.

Decisions regarding all these hyperparameters are commonly made by understanding their effect on the validation performance. The brute force empirical approach would be training the model repeatedly using different sets of hyperparameters on the training dataset and then observing the network performance on the validation dataset. After choosing the best model, it should be run on a yet another separately kept dataset called the test set. The performance of the network on the test set is the one that should be reported as a metric of evaluation for the deep neural network. To summarize, the training set is used to train the weights of the network by back-propagation, the validation set is used to tune the hyperparameters to obtain the optimal model configurations, and the test set is used to report the overall performance of the network. Ideally, the test set should never be used to tune hyperparameters as they serve as a method of evaluating a model that is ready for deployment.

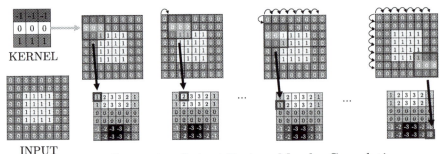

KERNEL

INPUT

Generating Output Feature Map by Convolution

Figure 3.3: The convolution operation.

3.3 Evolution of deep learning models and applications

The evolution of deep learning models started during the late 1990s with the introduction of convolutional neural networks. Since then, deep neural networks have been improved with several theoretical and practical upgrades. In what follows, we discuss some of the most influential concepts.

1) *Convolution:*
   Prior to the introduction of CNNs, automatic feature extraction from images were carried out by using fully connected layers across the entire span of the image. These kinds of methods worked satisfactorily for well-curated datasets like recognizing digits, where there is limited variance in the shape, size, and position of the objects. For unrestricted images, these networks fail miserably as they do not take into account the different shapes, sizes, and positions in which objects can occur in an image. The introduction of convolution [1] allowed kernel-based operations, where a small set of weights are shared across different parts of the image as shown in Fig. 3.3. This models the redundancy in the features to a great extent.

2) *Stacked convolutional layers:*
   Since single convolutional layers operate in a small field of view, which moves along the width and height of the image, they learn very low-level features like spots, lines and gradients. More complex features can be obtained in two ways. Firstly, by combining low-level features to detect more complex shapes such as polygons, curves, and textures, which then can further be combined to create even more complex features like various small parts of an object and so on. This can be achieved by stacking several convolutional layers [1] where each layers takes the features maps from the previous layer as shown in Fig. 3.4. The second aspect is a larger field of view to operate. As simple shapes are combined in a layer to form more complex structures, the kernels operating in

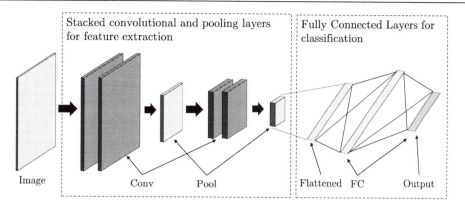

Stacked convolutional and pooling layers for feature extraction

Fully Connected Layers for classification

Image   Conv   Pool   Flattened FC   Output

Figure 3.4: Stacking layers for learning more complex features.

the layer should have a larger field of view to cover the entire structure. However, even though this can be done by increasing the kernel size, it would result in an increase in the number of parameters. A more appropriate way is to reduce the size of the feature map and use the same sized kernel as before, but it can span over a larger area corresponding to the original image. This type of subsampling operations is carried out by the pooling layer.

3) *Greedy layerwise training:*
   Although it became quite clear that depth in the network is necessary for learning complex features, training too many layers can hinder the training process. This hindrance can be either due to lack of computational resources or due to factors like vanishing gradients. A common approach to address this issue was training the network in a greedy layerwise fashion [8,21]. Using this process the training can start with a single feature extracting layer connected to the output layer. After training that single layer, the output layer can be unplugged. A new hidden layer and output layer can be connected, and the network can be trained again while freezing the previously trained layers as shown in Fig. 3.5. This process can be repeated multiple times, and one hidden layer can be added each time. This allows very deep networks to be trained without the impact of vanishing gradients and also training only a part of the total number of parameters at a time.

4) *Rectified linear units:*
   Although sigmoid and tanh activations are great for bounded outputs, their gradients tend to zero as one moves toward either extremities. This hinders the learning process in the later stages of the training. Using too many back-to-back sigmoid or tanh activations results in vanishing gradients, which is caused due to successive multiplication of very small partial derivatives (as necessary during back-propagation). Rectified linear units [22,23] brought a new concept to the table where negative features are set to zero

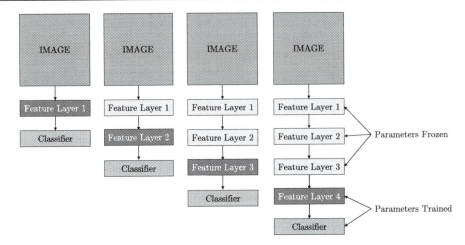

Figure 3.5: A demonstration of greedy layerwise training where layers are trained and more layers are added incrementally.

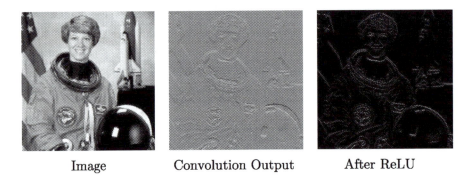

Image   Convolution Output   After ReLU

Figure 3.6: The effect of rectified linear units on convolution outputs.

and positive features are kept as it is as shown in Fig. 3.6. This brings a nonaffine transformation in the feature space, thus introducing nonlinearity into the system. Moreover, this results in a zero gradient for negative outputs and a unit gradient for positive output, which is great for building deep networks as vanishing gradients can be avoided.

5) *Scale space pyramid:*

As more deep networks were being explored, a common principle for building layers was implementing a scale space pyramid. This emphasizes to arrange layers such that earlier feature extracting layers have lower number of kernels operating with a small field of view to learn a handful of the most basic features that can be used later to construct a large number of features. As we progress down the depth of the network, subsampling layers reduce the feature maps size and increase the field of view of the

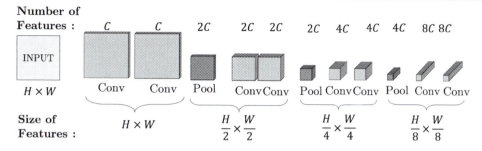

Figure 3.7: Organizing layers as scale space pyramid.

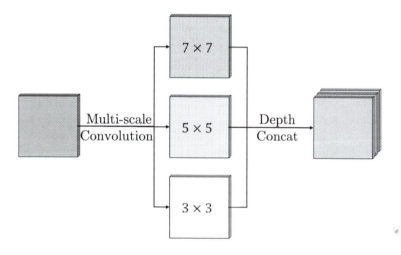

Figure 3.8: Parallel branches with multiscale convolutions.

kernels. Moreover, as the width and height of the feature maps decrease, the number of channels increases to encode more and more complex concepts. This is called a scale space pyramid [8], where the earlier layers form the base of the pyramid with few number of kernels operating with a small field of view to create large feature maps, and the later layers form the tip with high number of kernels operating on a larger field of view to create smaller feature maps (see Fig. 3.7).

6) *Multiscale convolutions:*

Another common approach to increase the learning capability of networks is using kernels of different sizes in the same layer to extract multiscale features. This can be implemented as parallel branches in small convolution blocks [9], or even entire columns of feature extractors [24] can be operated with different configurations. In cases like these, features from each branch or columns are concatenated at the end before passing to the next layer or the output layer as shown in Fig. 3.8.

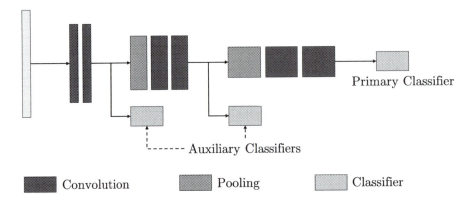

Primary Classifier

Auxiliary Classifiers

Convolution   Pooling   Classifier

Figure 3.9: Auxiliary classifiers for gradient boosting.

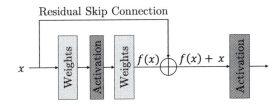

Figure 3.10: Residual block.

7) *Auxiliary classifiers:*
   As the depth of the networks kept on increasing, the distance between the initial layers and the output layer increased. The effect of the output layer on the earlier layers kept on decreasing. To address this issue and facilitate better gradient propagation to the earlier layers, auxiliary classifiers were attached to intermediate features of the network to increase the impact of the objective function in the earlier layers [9]. It is graphically illustrated in Fig. 3.9.

8) *Residual connections:*
   Though auxiliary classifiers can facilitate better gradient propagation in earlier layers, it requires additional neurons and additional hyperparameter tuning to determine ideal location for gradients. Residual connections [10], on the other hand, provide a much easier solution by adding a parallel shortcut branch across a couple of convolutional layers that contains no any weights. This short cut branch allows every layer to have a direct connection to the output layer. This allowed researchers to build networks with hundreds of layers without any kind of gradient-related issues (see Fig. 3.10).

9) *Kernel factorization:*
   Kernel factorization is a way of reducing the number of parameters while mimicing the learning capability of larger kernels. Spatial factorization [25] factorizes the kernel in

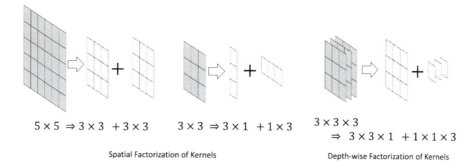

$5 \times 5 \Rightarrow 3 \times 3 + 3 \times 3$ $\qquad$ $3 \times 3 \Rightarrow 3 \times 1 + 1 \times 3$ $\qquad$ $3 \times 3 \times 3$
$\Rightarrow 3 \times 3 \times 1 + 1 \times 1 \times 3$

Spatial Factorization of Kernels $\qquad\qquad\qquad\qquad$ Depth-wise Factorization of Kernels

Figure 3.11: Kernel factorizations.

terms of height and width. For example, a 5×5 convolution with 25 parameters can be factorized to two cascaded 3×3 kernels with a total of 18 parameters. Furthermore, 3×3 kernels can be factorized into 1×3 and 3×1 convolutions. Factorization can also be carried out across channels by using depthwise separable convolutions [26]. In a depthwise separable convolution, two separate operations are performed. Firstly, a spatial convolution operation is performed independently over each channel of the input tensor sharing the same single depth kernel over all the channels. After that, the number of input channels should be equal to the number of output channels. This is followed by a pixelwise convolution with a 1×1 kernel, projecting the features computed by the previous step onto a new feature space (Fig. 3.11).

10) *Attention:*

Humans have a innate ability to focus their attention on specific concepts necessary to address a problem. This can be mimicked in deep neural networks by using neurons that can decide to attend specific features [27]. Attention can be achieved by neurons that learn weights bounded by sigmoid activation. These weights can be multiplied with learned features to mask out unnecessary concepts. Attention has several applications in areas like neural excitation [28], visual attention [29], and so on.

11) *Transposed convolution:*

Transposed convolution, also known as convolution with fractional strides, has been introduced to reverse the effects of a traditional convolution operation. It is often referred to as deconvolution [30]. However, deconvolution, as defined in signal processing, is different from transposed convolution in terms of the basic formulation, although they effectively address the same problem. In a convolution operation, there is a change in size of the input based on the amount of padding and stride of the kernels. A stride of 2 will create half the number of activations as that of a stride of 1. For a transposed convolution to work, padding and stride should be controlled in a way that the size change is reversed. This is achieved by dilating the input space. As shown in Fig. 3.12, with the

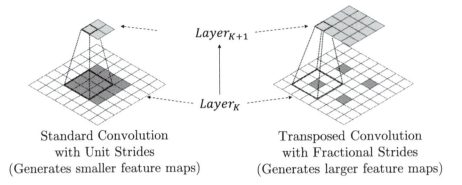

Standard Convolution   Transposed Convolution
with Unit Strides   with Fractional Strides
(Generates smaller feature maps) (Generates larger feature maps)

Figure 3.12: Transposed convolutions.

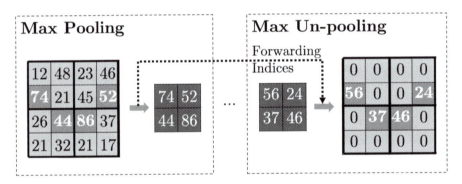

Figure 3.13: Unpooling.

inputs dilated by a fixed amount, the number of activations are multiplied because the kernel has to produce activations in more positions. This method is common where we need to reverse the effect of convolutions with strides or subsampling operations to create higher-resolution feature maps from lower-resolution ones. This is commonly used in encoder–decoder architectures for segmentation [31].

12) *Segmentation:*

Another approach to reduce the size of the activations is through pooling layers. A 2x2 pooling layer with a stride of two reduces the height and width of the image by a factor of 2. In such a pooling layer a 2x2 neighborhood of a pixel is compressed to a single pixel. Different types of pooling performs the compression in different ways. Max-pooling considers the maximum activation value among 4 pixels, whereas average pooling takes an average of the same. As shown in Fig. 3.13, the corresponding un-pooling layer decompresses a single pixel to a neighborhood of 2x2 pixels to double the height and width of the image. This can be achieved by either copying the same value to multiple positioned in the upsampled feature map or copying it to one of the positions, whereas the rest pixels are kept as zeros. These filler values are computed in succeeding convolutional layers [31,32].

Over the last couple of decades, deep learning has inspired several approaches in different areas of computer vision, such as classification, localization, and segmentation. Some of the most common deep neural networks in these areas are listed in the following section.

3.3.1 Classification

Image classification is one of the most common application areas in the field of computer vision. CNNs perform image classification by using a series of feature extraction layers and a classification layer at the end. CNNs have gone through several upgrades over the years (medical imaging [33]). For example, different classification deep learning models were applied for COVID-19 screening purpose [34–41].

In what follows, we discuss a few commonly used models.

1) *LeNet5:*

The introduction of convolution and pooling brought a huge shift in the field of computer vision. This started when the LeNet5 [1] network was proposed. In today's standard, LeNet5 is trivial but is the foundation of CNNs. The LeNet5 was designed for processing handwritten digits. It accepts an input of 32×32. The first layer consists of 6 feature extracting kernels of size 9×9. Each of these produces 6 28×28 feature maps. Following this a subsampling layer reduces the feature map to 14×14 using max-pooling. A second feature extraction layer containing 16 9×9 kernels, each producing a 10×10 feature map. A subsampling layer reduces the features to 5×5. This concludes the feature extracting layer. All activations from the $16 \times 5 \times 5$ block is flattened to create a linear vector. A series of 3 fully connected layers with 120, 84, and 10 neurons maps these features to a 10-dimensional logit vector. A cross entropy error is reduced with the help of stochastic gradient descent. LeNet5 proved to be one of the most efficient image classification approaches capable of automatic extracting a set of features from the image. The architecture is shown in Fig. 3.14.

2) *AlexNet:*

One of the most challenging datasets in the field of computer vision was the ImageNet. A global challenge called the ImageNet Large-Scale Visual Recognition Competition, invited researchers all around the world solve this massive 1000 class image classification problem by processing over a million images. CNNs made a massive mark when the AlexNet [2] benched an impressive 0.15 top-5 error rate. This is when CNNs were recognized as a potent tool for large-scale computer vision problems. They were built upon the LeNet architecture by increasing the depth to include 5 feature extracting convolution

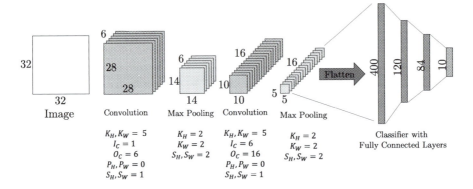

Figure 3.14: LeNet5 architecture.

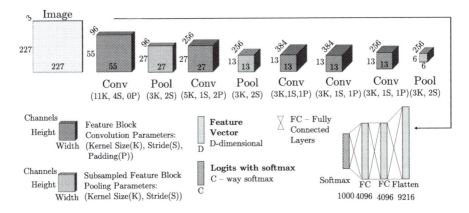

Figure 3.15: AlexNet architecture.

layers followed by 3 fully connected layers to output a 1000-dimensional softmax distribution. Some of the key innovation in AlexNet was the implementation of Rectified linear units, which allowed deeper networks to be trained without experiencing vanishing gradients. Another innovation was the introduction of local response normalization to prevent neurons for saturating too soon for efficient learning. This architecture was made more efficient by splitting spatial convolution filters into a set of spatial and pointwise filters in the SqueezeNet architecture. This resulted in a lower number of neurons without reduction in the performance. The architecture is shown in Fig. 3.15.

3) *VGGNet:*

The visual geometry group at Oxford University is well known for its works in generic computer vision problems. In the domain of CNNs, one of the most significant contributions was the VGGNet [8]. Till this date the philosophy behind VGGNet serves as a template for building CNN models. VGGNet proposed an expandable CNN that consisted

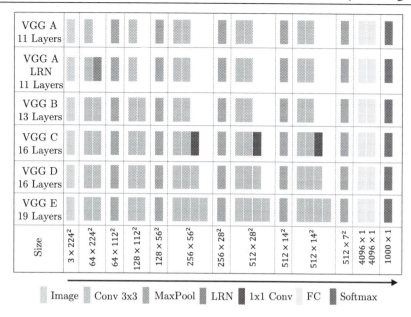

Figure 3.16: VGGNet: Each row shows a variation of the VGGNet.

of convolutional blocks. Each convolutional block contains a number of convolutional layers. As shown in Fig. 3.16, the specific number of layers can be varied depending on complexity of concepts we wish to learn. Between each block, there is a max-pooling layer that subsamples the features by a factor of two and increases the number of channels to accommodate more complex features. With this feature, an array of CNNs was proposed, ranging from 11 layer up to 19 layers. Increasing the depth of network allowed the network to represent complex features; however, the gradient propagation was affected due to vanishing gradients.

4) *GoogLeNet and the Inception family:*

The kernel sizes of CNNs play an important role in the feature extraction process. Most of the early networks used a single kernel size per layer. When the GoogLeNet [9] was introduced, most of the competing CNNs were linear cascades of feature extractors. The idea of GoogLeNet was exploring deeper and wider options. In terms of width, GoogLeNet implemented something called an inception module, which is parallel feature extraction pipeline involving kernels of different sizes. Feature maps from each branch were depth concatenated to form a combined feature, which was passed to the next layer. Another important feature was the global average pooling, which reduced feature maps of the last layers to scalars by conducting a full scale average pooling with a kernel of same size as that of the image. Unlike AlexNet, GoogLeNet only had a single fully connected layer. Almost 94% of AlexNet's parameters came from the 3 fully connected layers, which was

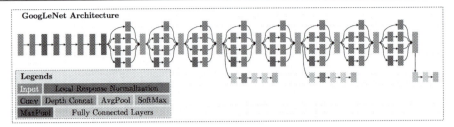

Figure 3.17: GoogLeNet.

avoided in the GoogLeNet. To facilitate a better gradient flow, one or more auxiliary classifiers were connected to the intermediate layers, which serve as gradient boosters. The GoogLeNet model was later extended in several versions under the name of Inception Net. In the extensions, several new concepts, such as batch normalization and kernel factorizations, were introduced [25], which were responsible for better regularization and parameter compression, respectively. The architecture is shown in Fig. 3.17.

5) *ResNet family:*

With the success of CNNs like AlexNet, VGGNet, and GoogLeNet, it was evident that deep neural networks were the way to go for learning complex visual concepts. However, increasing depth cannot be achieved by simply stacking layers on top of each other. It came with difficulties in the flow of gradients. Long chains of gradients often ended up reducing long distance gradients to almost zero. Each of the previously mentioned CNNs added depth to the network by introducing some feature to deal with the vanishing gradients such as rectified linear units, layerwise training, or auxiliary classifiers. However, there was no effective generalized solution that could remove this issue of vanishing gradients altogether. To answer this issue, the residual networks [10] were proposed. The key feature of a residual networks was an identity shortcut connection that skips over one or more layers and adds to the output. If a standard set of layers is represented by a function $\mathcal{F}$ that works on the input x, with a residual connection, then the output would be $\mathcal{F}(x) + x$ instead of $\mathcal{F}(x)$. This small update allowed gradients to split in the addition layer during back-propagation when a copy of the gradients skips over all the intermediate layers to reach the earlier layers, and this identity branch does not diminish the value of gradient by any kind of operation. This upgrade allowed very deep networks to be built, which had hundreds and thousands of layers. There have been several upgrades over the ResNet model. One upgrade was to involve multiscale kernels like the inception net. This network was codenamed as ResNeXt. Further, down the line, densely connected layers were implemented under the name of DenseNet, which increased the number of shortcut connections by allowing shortcut connections not only across a few layers but having multiple shortcut connections from one layer to several layers succeeding it. The architecture of ResNet is shown in Fig. 3.18.

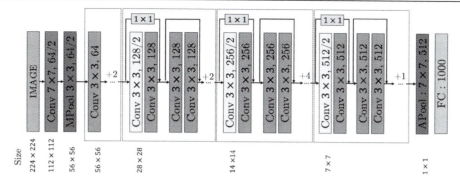

Figure 3.18: Residual networks.

3.3.2 Localization

Whereas classification algorithms are designed to answer the "what" question when it comes to visual understanding, localization algorithms answer the "where" question. In most cases, localization techniques involve prediction of bounding boxes denoting the location of desired objects. We discuss some of the most common approaches.

1) *Region-based CNN (R-CNN):*
    The introduction of the CNNs raised many new questions in the domain of computer vision, one of them primarily being whether a network like AlexNet can be extended to detect the presence of more than one object. R-CNNs [42] used selective search technique to propose probable object regions and performed classification on the cropped window to verify sensible localization based on the output probability distribution. Selective search technique analyzes various aspects like texture, color, or intensities to cluster the pixels into objects. The bounding boxes corresponding 10 to these segments are passed through classifying networks to short-list some of the most sensible boxes. Finally, with a simple linear regression network, a tighter coordinate can be obtained. The main downside of the technique is its computational cost. The network needs to compute a forward pass for every bounding box proposition. The problem with sharing computation across all boxes was that the boxes were of different sizes and hence uniform sized features were not achievable. In the upgraded fast R-CNN [43], ROI (Region of Interest) Pooling was proposed, in which the region of interests was dynamically pooled to obtain a fixed-size feature output. Henceforth, the network was mainly bottlenecked by the selective search technique for candidate region proposal. In faster R-CNN [44], instead of depending on external features, the intermediate activation maps were used to propose bounding boxes, thus speeding up the feature extraction process. Bounding boxes are representatives of the location of the object; however, they do not provide pixel-level segments. A faster R-CNN

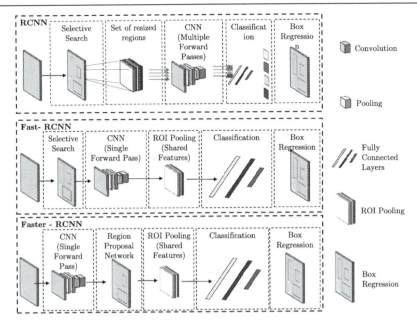

Figure 3.19: Object localization with R-CNN, fast R-CNN and faster R-CNN.

network was later extended as Mask R-CNN [45] with parallel branch, which performed pixel-level object-specific binary classification to provide accurate segments. Region proposal networks have often been combined with other networks to give instance-level segmentation. RCNN was further improved under the name of HyperNet by using features from multiple layers of the feature extractor. Region proposal networks have also been implemented for instance-specific segmentation as well. As mentioned before, object detection capabilities of approaches like RCNN are often coupled with segmentation models to generate different masks for different instances of the same object. The architectures of the R-CNNs are shown in Fig. 3.19.

2) *You Only Look Once (YOLO):*
R-CNN visualized the localization problem as a sequence of location prediction, verification, and regression operations. This came with several costs such as the overhead and viability of proposing candidate boxes, multiple pass of the network for box verification and then followed by a regression operation for fine-tuning. The philosophy of YOLO [46] is treating the object localization as a classification problem so that a single pass would be enough to detect the position of the boxes. In the YOLO network the image was divided into different grids. For each grid, there is a set of classifiers, which detects whether the centroid of a region of interest is present in the grid or not. For an activated gradient, a set of predefined anchor boxes are aligned to the center of the grid. Finally,

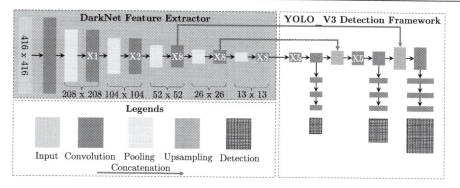

Figure 3.20: The YOLOv3 model for object localization.

a regression network fine tunes the anchor box to refine it fit the object perfectly. This algorithm was soon updated to incorporate multiscale detection by classifying grids of different sizes [47,48]. The YOLO network has been one of the most successful applications of object detection. The architecture of YOLOv3 is shown in Fig. 3.20.

3.3.3 Segmentation

Localization techniques like R-CNN and YOLO do a decent job of finding the approximate location of objects in an image, but the information is represented only by a bounding box. However, human beings are much more capable of identifying distinct objects with extreme precision. Segmentation algorithms aim to achieve that by performing pixel level classification. They have tremendous applications in fields like medical imaging for detecting various parts of organs with pixel-level precision. We discuss some common approaches to segmentation.

1) *Fully convolutional networks for segmentation:*
   Classification tasks generally combine a set of convolutional feature extractors followed by a fully connected classifier. However, the fully connected layers at the end fail to preserve spatial information encoded in the feature maps. For segmentation algorithms, such fully connected layers are hence avoided as pixel-level features are essential for semantic segmentation. One way to avoid fully connected linear layers is the use of a full-size average pooling to convert a set of two-dimensional activation maps to a set of scalar values. As these pooled scalars are connected to the output layers, the weights corresponding to each class may be used to perform weighted summation of the corresponding activation maps in the previous layers. This process, called Global Average Pooling (GAP) [9], can be directly used on various trained networks like residual network to and object-specific activation zones, which can be used for pixel-level segmentation. The major issue with

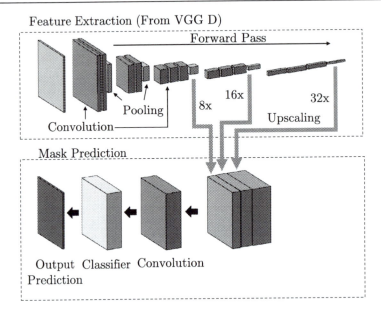

Figure 3.21: Fully connected network (FCN).

such a algorithm is the loss of sharpness due to the intermediate subsampling operations. Subsampling is a common operation in convolutional neural networks to increase
the sensory area of kernels. This means that as the activations maps reduce in size in the
subsequent layers, the kernels convoluting over them actually correspond to a larger area
in the original image. However, they reduce the image size in the process, which when
up-sampled to original size, loses sharpness. The most common approach to deal with
this is incorporating features from layers of different resolutions, which aid in making the
segments sharper [4]. Another approach, called the pyramid scene parsing network [49],
was built upon the FCN-based pixel-level classification network. The feature maps from a
ResNet-101 network are converted to activations of different resolutions thorough multiscale pooling layers, which are later upsampled and concatenated with the original feature
map to perform segmentation. The different types of pooling modules focus on different
areas of the activation map. Pooling kernels of various sizes like $1 \times 1, 2 \times 2, 3 \times 3, 6 \times 6$
look into different areas of the activation map to create the spatial pooling pyramid. The
architecture of FCN is shown in Fig. 3.21.

2) *Encoder–decoder architectures:*
Whereas features from multiple layers can be upsampled accordingly and concatenated,
a more sensible approach would be running convolutional layers to refine in each step of
the segment construction process. This is where encoder–decoder architectures come into

play. Autoencoders have been traditionally used for feature extraction from input samples while trying to retain most of the original information. An autoencoder is basically composed of an encoder, which encodes the input representations from a raw input to a possibly lower-dimensional intermediate representation, and a decoder, which attempts to reconstruct the original input from the intermediate representation. The loss is computed in terms of the difference between the raw input images and the reconstructed output image. The generative nature of the decoder part has often been modified and used for image segmentation purposes. Unlike the traditional autoencoders, during segmentation, the loss is computed in terms of the difference between the reconstructed pixel-level class distribution and the desired pixel-level class distribution. One benefit of encoder–decoder architectures is that they can be designed to handle any size of input (with minimal restrictions) and produce a segmentation of the same resolution. These models are easy to design, train, and deploy. There are several implementations following this philosophy, and we discuss some of them.

a) *SegNet:*

Max-pooling has been the most commonly used technique for reducing the size of the activation maps for various reasons. The activations represent the response of the region of an image to a specific kernel. In max-pooling a region of pixels is compressed to single value by considering only the maximum response obtained within that region. If a typical autoencoder compresses a 2×2 neighborhood of pixels to a single pixel in the encoding phase, the decoder must decompress the pixel to a similar dimension of 2×2. By forwarding pooling indices the network basically remembers the location of the maximum value among the 4 pixels while performing max-pooling. The index corresponding to the maximum value is forwarded to the decoder so that while the un-pooling operation the value from the single pixel can be copied to the corresponding location in 2×2 region in the next layer. The values in the remaining three positions are computed in the subsequent convolutional layers. If the value was copied to random location without the knowledge of the pooling indices, there would be inconsistencies in classification, especially in the boundary regions. This method is the key behind the SegNet network [32]. The SegNet algorithm was launched in 2015 to compete with the FCN network on complex indoor and outdoor images. The architecture was composed of 5 encoding blocks and 5 decoding blocks. The encoding blocks followed the architecture of the feature extractor in VGG-16 network. Each block is a sequence of multiple convolution, batch normalization, and ReLU layers. Each encoding block ends with a max-pooling layer where the indices are stored. Each decoding block begins with an unpooling layer where the saved pooling indices are used. The indices from the max-pooling layer of the ith block in the encoder are forwarded to the max-unpooling layer in the (L_{i+1})th block in the decoder, where L is the total number of blocks in each encoder or decoder. This is shown in Fig. 3.22.

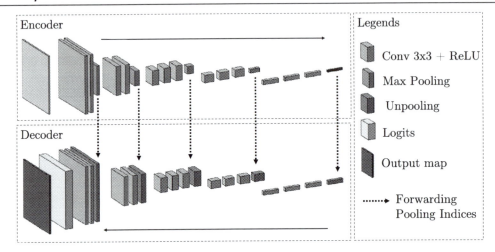

Figure 3.22: SegNet.

b) *UNet:*

The U-Net architecture [50], proposed in 2015, proved to be quite efficient for a variety of problems such as segmentation of neuronal structures, radiography, and cell tracking challenges. The network is characterized by an encoder with a series of convolutions and max-pooling layers. The decoding layer contains a mirrored sequence of convolutions and transposed convolutions. As described till now, it behaves as a traditional autoencoder. Previously, it has been mentioned how the level of abstraction plays an important role in the quality of image segmentation. To consider various levels of abstraction, U-Net implements skip connections to copy the uncompressed activations from encoding blocks to their mirrored counterparts among the decoding blocks. The model is shown in Fig. 3.23. The feature extractor of the U-Net can also be upgraded to provide better segmentation maps. The network nicknamed "The one hundred layers Tiramisu" [51] applied the concept of U-Net using a dense-net-based feature extractor.

c) *SegFast:*

The SegFast network [52,53] built on the already existing robust encoder–decoder models by making them more efficient. The SegFast draws inspiration from other CNNs like the SqueezeNet [54], which reduced the number of parameters of AlexNet by splitting spatial operations into a set of pointwise spatial convolutions. SegFast further made it faster by replacing the standard spatial convolutions by depthwise convolutions. SegFast follows a similar principle as U-Net but achieves similar level of performance using much lesser number of parameters. The SegFast model has also been used in several other domains [55,56]. The model is shown in Fig. 3.24.

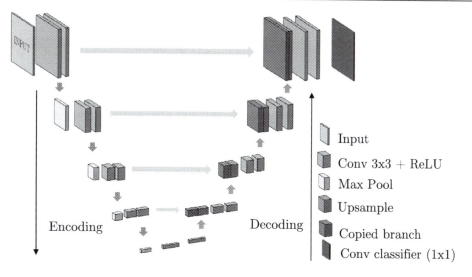

Figure 3.23: UNet.

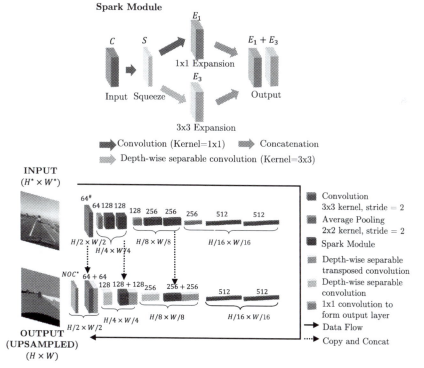

$NOC^* =$ No. of classes, $H^* =$ Height, $W^* =$ Width, $C^\#$: Number of channels

Figure 3.24: Spark modules and SegFast.

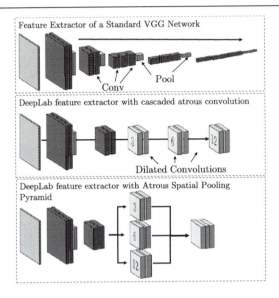

Figure 3.25: DeepLab.

3) *DeepLab:*

Although pixel-level segmentation was effective, two complementing issues were still affecting the performance. Firstly, smaller kernel sizes failed to capture contextual information. In classification problems, this is handled using pooling layers that increase the sensory area of the kernels with respect to the original image but in segmentation that reduces the sharpness of the segmented output. Alternative usage of larger kernels tends to be slower due to significantly larger number of trainable parameters. To handle this issue, the DeepLab family of algorithms [57] demonstrated the usage of various methodologies like atrous convolutions [58], spatial pooling pyramids, and fully connected conditional random fields [59] to perform image segmentation with great efficiency. The network is shown in Fig. 3.25.

a) *Atrous/Dilated convolution:*

The size of the convolution kernels in any layer determines the sensory response area of the network. Whereas smaller kernels extract local information, larger kernels try to focus on more contextual information. However, larger kernels normally come with greater number of parameters. For example, to have a sensory region of 6 × 6, we must have 36 neurons. To reduce the number of parameters in the CNN, the sensory area is increased in higher layers through techniques like pooling. Pooling layers reduce the size of the image. When an image is pooled by a 2x2 kernel with a stride of two, the size of the image reduces by 25%. A kernel with an area of 3x3 corresponds to a larger sensory area of 6 × 6 in the original image. However, unlike before, now

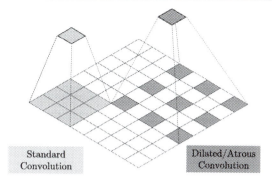

Figure 3.26: Atrous convolutions.

only 18 neurons (9 for each layer) are needed in the convolution kernel. In case of
segmentation, pooling creates new problems. The reduction in the image size results
in loss of sharpness in generated segments as the reduced maps are scaled up to image
size. To deal with these two issues simultaneously, dilated or atrous convolutions [58]
play a key role. Atrous/dilated convolutions increase the field of view without increasing the number of parameters. A 3x3 kernel with a dilation factor of 1 can act upon
an area of 5×5 in the image. Each row and column of the kernel has three neurons,
which is multiplied with intensity values in the image separated by the dilation factor
of 1. In this way the kernels can span over larger areas while keeping the number of
neurons low and also preserving the sharpness of the image (see Fig. 3.26).

b) *Spatial pyramid pooling:*
Spatial pyramid pooling was introduced in R-CNN [42], where ROI pooling showed
the benefit of using multiscale regions for object localization. However, in DeepLab,
atrous convolutions were preferred over pooling layers for changing the field of view
or sensory area. To imitate the effect of ROI pooling, multiple branches with atrous
convolutions of different dilations were combined together to utilize multiscale properties for image segmentation.

c) *Fully connected conditional random field:*
A conditional random field is an undirected discriminative probabilistic graphical
model often used for various sequence learning problems. Unlike discrete classifiers,
while classifying a sample, it takes into account the labels of other neighboring samples. Image segmentation can be treated as a sequence of pixel classifications. The
label of a pixel is not only dependent on its own intensity values but also on the values of neighboring pixels. This model can be plugged as boundary refinement module
into any segmentation algorithms as shown in Fig. 3.27. This basically reclassifies
misclassified by analyzing intensity and predicted classes of other pixels around
it [59].

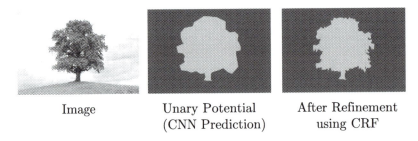

Image   Unary Potential   After Refinement
(CNN Prediction)   using CRF

Figure 3.27: An example of boundary refinement by conditional random fields.

References

[1] Yann LeCun, Léon Bottou, Yoshua Bengio, Patrick Haffner, Gradient-based learning applied to document recognition, Proceedings of the IEEE 86 (11) (1998) 2278–2324.

[2] Alex Krizhevsky, Ilya Sutskever, Geoffrey E. Hinton, ImageNet classification with deep convolutional neural networks, in: Advances in Neural Information Processing Systems, 2012, pp. 1097–1105.

[3] Sara Sabour, Nicholas Frosst, Geoffrey E. Hinton, Dynamic routing between capsules, in: Advances in Neural Information Processing Systems, 2017, pp. 3856–3866.

[4] Jonathan Long, Evan Shelhamer, Trevor Darrell, Fully convolutional networks for semantic segmentation, in: Proceedings of the IEEE Conference on Computer Vision and Pattern Recognition, 2015, pp. 3431–3440.

[5] Mark A. Kramer, Autoassociative neural networks, Computers & Chemical Engineering 16 (4) (1992) 313–328.

[6] Leslie Pack Kaelbling, Michael L. Littman, Andrew W. Moore, Reinforcement learning: a survey, Journal of Artificial Intelligence Research 4 (1996) 237–285.

[7] Ozan Sener, Vladlen Koltun, Multi-task learning as multi-objective optimization, in: Advances in Neural Information Processing Systems, 2018, pp. 527–538.

[8] Karen Simonyan, Andrew Zisserman, Very deep convolutional networks for large-scale image recognition, preprint, arXiv:1409.1556, 2014.

[9] Christian Szegedy, Wei Liu, Yangqing Jia, Pierre Sermanet, Scott Reed, Dragomir Anguelov, Dumitru Erhan, Vincent Vanhoucke, Andrew Rabinovich, Going deeper with convolutions, in: Proceedings of the IEEE Conference on Computer Vision and Pattern Recognition, 2015, pp. 1–9.

[10] Kaiming He, Xiangyu Zhang, Shaoqing Ren, Jian Sun, Deep residual learning for image recognition, in: Proceedings of the IEEE Conference on Computer Vision and Pattern Recognition, 2016, pp. 770–778.

[11] Gao Huang, Zhuang Liu, Laurens Van Der Maaten, Kilian Q. Weinberger, Densely connected convolutional networks, in: Proceedings of the IEEE Conference on Computer Vision and Pattern Recognition, 2017, pp. 4700–4708.

[12] Dan Cireşan, Ueli Meier, Jonathan Masci, Jürgen Schmidhuber, Multi-column deep neural network for traffic sign classification, Neural Networks 32 (2012) 333–338.

[13] Dan Cireşan, Ueli Meier, Jürgen Schmidhuber, Multi-column deep neural networks for image classification, in: 2012 IEEE Conference on Computer Vision and Pattern Recognition, IEEE, 2012, pp. 3642–3649.

[14] Ritesh Sarkhel, Nibaran Das, Aritra Das, Mahantapas Kundu, Mita Nasipuri, A multi-scale deep quad tree based feature extraction method for the recognition of isolated handwritten characters of popular indic scripts, Pattern Recognition 71 (2017) 78–93.

[15] Bodhisatwa Mandal, Ritesh Sarkhel, Swarnendu Ghosh, Nibaran Das, Mita Nasipuri, Two-phase dynamic routing for micro and macro-level equivariance in multi-column capsule networks, Pattern Recognition (2020) 107595.

[16] Soumya Ukil, Swarnendu Ghosh, Sk Md Obaidullah, KC Santosh, Kaushik Roy, Nibaran Das, Improved word-level handwritten indic script identification by integrating small convolutional neural networks, Neural Computing and Applications (2019) 1–16.

[17] Swarnendu Ghosh, Nibaran Das, Mita Nasipuri, Reshaping inputs for convolutional neural network: some common and uncommon methods, Pattern Recognition 93 (2019) 79–94.

[18] Connor Shorten, Taghi M. Khoshgoftaar, A survey on image data augmentation for deep learning, Journal of Big Data 6 (1) (2019) 60.

[19] Yann LeCun, Corinna Cortes, Christopher J.C. Burges, The MNIST database of handwritten digits 10 (34) (1998) 14, http://yann.lecun.com/exdb/mnist, 1998.

[20] Alex Krizhevsky, Vinod Nair, Geoffrey Hinton, The CIFAR-10 dataset, online: http://www.cs.toronto.edu/kriz/cifar.html, 2014, 55.

[21] Yoshua Bengio, Pascal Lamblin, Dan Popovici, Hugo Larochelle, Greedy layer-wise training of deep networks, in: Advances in Neural Information Processing Systems, 2007, pp. 153–160.

[22] Vinod Nair, Geoffrey E. Hinton, Rectified linear units improve restricted Boltzmann machines, in: ICML, 2010.

[23] Xavier Glorot, Antoine Bordes, Yoshua Bengio, Deep sparse rectifier neural networks, in: Proceedings of the 14th International Conference on Artificial Intelligence and Statistics, 2011, pp. 315–323.

[24] Aritra Das, Swarnendu Ghosh, Ritesh Sarkhel, Sandipan Choudhuri, Nibaran Das, Mita Nasipuri, Combining multilevel contexts of superpixel using convolutional neural networks to perform natural scene labeling, in: Recent Developments in Machine Learning and Data Analytics, Springer, 2019, pp. 297–306.

[25] Christian Szegedy, Vincent Vanhoucke, Sergey Ioffe, Jon Shlens, Zbigniew Wojna, Rethinking the inception architecture for computer vision, in: Proceedings of the IEEE Conference on Computer Vision and Pattern Recognition, 2016, pp. 2818–2826.

[26] François Chollet, Xception: deep learning with depthwise separable convolutions, in: Proceedings of the IEEE Conference on Computer Vision and Pattern Recognition, 2017, pp. 1251–1258.

[27] Ashish Vaswani, Noam Shazeer, Niki Parmar, Jakob Uszkoreit, Llion Jones, Aidan N. Gomez, Łukasz Kaiser, Illia Polosukhin, Attention is all you need, in: Advances in Neural Information Processing Systems, 2017, pp. 5998–6008.

[28] Jie Hu, Li Shen, Gang Sun, Squeeze-and-excitation networks, in: Proceedings of the IEEE Conference on Computer Vision and Pattern Recognition, 2018, pp. 7132–7141.

[29] Kelvin Xu, Jimmy Ba, Ryan Kiros, Kyunghyun Cho, Aaron Courville, Ruslan Salakhudinov, Rich Zemel, Yoshua Bengio, Show, attend and tell: neural image caption generation with visual attention, in: International Conference on Machine Learning, 2015, pp. 2048–2057.

[30] Matthew D. Zeiler, Dilip Krishnan, Graham W. Taylor, Rob Fergus, Deconvolutional networks, in: 2010 IEEE Computer Society Conference on Computer Vision and Pattern Recognition, IEEE, 2010, pp. 2528–2535.

[31] Hyeonwoo Noh, Seunghoon Hong, Bohyung Han, Learning deconvolution network for semantic segmentation, in: Proceedings of the IEEE International Conference on Computer Vision, 2015, pp. 1520–1528.

[32] Vijay Badrinarayanan, Alex Kendall, Roberto Cipolla, Segnet: a deep convolutional encoder–decoder architecture for image segmentation, IEEE Transactions on Pattern Analysis and Machine Intelligence 39 (12) (2017) 2481–2495.

[33] KC Santosh, S. Antani, D.S. Guru, N. Dey, Medical Imaging: Artificial Intelligence, Image Recognition, and Machine Learning Techniques, 1st ed., MCRC Press, 2019.

[34] KC Santosh, Ai-driven tools for coronavirus outbreak: need of active learning and cross-population train/test models on multitudinal/multimodal data, Journal of Medical Systems 44 (5) (2020) 93, https://doi.org/10.1007/s10916-020-01562-1.

[35] KC Santosh, Sourodip Ghosh, Covid-19 imaging tools: how big data is big?, Journal of Medical Systems 45 (7) (2021) 71, https://doi.org/10.1007/s10916-021-01747-2.

[36] Dipayan Das, KC Santosh, Umapada Pal, Truncated inception net: Covid-19 outbreak screening using chest X-rays, Physical Engineering Sciences in Medicine 8 (2020) 1–11, https://doi.org/10.1007/s13246-020-00888-x.

[37] KC Santosh, COVID-19 prediction models and unexploited data, Journal of Medical Systems 44 (9) (2020) 170, https://doi.org/10.1007/s10916-020-01645-z.

[38] H. Mukherjee, S. Ghosh, A. Dhar, S.M. Obaidullah, KC Santosh, K. Roy, Deep neural network to detect COVID-19: one architecture for both CT scans and chest X-rays, Applied Intelligence 51 (2021) 2777–2789, https://doi.org/10.1007/s10489-020-01943-6.

[39] H. Mukherjee, A. Dhar, S.M. Obaidullah, KC Santosh, K. Roy, Shallow convolutional neural network for Covid-19 outbreak screening using chest X-rays, in: Cognitive Computation, 2021, https://doi.org/10.1007/s12559-020-09775-9.

[40] KC Santosh, Amit Joshi, Covid-19: Prediction, Decision-Making, and Its Impacts, Lecture Notes on Data Engineering and Communications Technologies, 2020.

[41] Amit Joshi, Nilanjan Dey, KC Santosh, Intelligent Systems and Methods to Combat Covid-19, Springer Briefs in Computational Intelligence, 2020.

[42] Ross Girshick, Jeff Donahue, Trevor Darrell, Jitendra Malik, Rich feature hierarchies for accurate object detection and semantic segmentation, in: Proceedings of the IEEE Conference on Computer Vision and Pattern Recognition, 2014, pp. 580–587.

[43] Ross Girshick, Fast R-CNN, in: Proceedings of the IEEE International Conference on Computer Vision, 2015, pp. 1440–1448.

[44] Shaoqing Ren, Kaiming He, Ross Girshick, Jian Sun, Faster R-CNN: towards real-time object detection with region proposal networks, in: Advances in Neural Information Processing Systems, 2015, pp. 91–99.

[45] Kaiming He, Georgia Gkioxari, Piotr Dollár, Ross Girshick, Mask R-CNN, in: Proceedings of the IEEE International Conference on Computer Vision, 2017, pp. 2961–2969.

[46] Joseph Redmon, Santosh Divvala, Ross Girshick, Ali Farhadi, You only look once: unified, real-time object detection, in: Proceedings of the IEEE Conference on Computer Vision and Pattern Recognition, 2016, pp. 779–788.

[47] Joseph Redmon, Ali Farhadi, YOLO9000: better, faster, stronger, in: Proceedings of the IEEE Conference on Computer Vision and Pattern Recognition, 2017, pp. 7263–7271.

[48] Joseph Redmon, Ali Farhadi, Yolov3: an incremental improvement, preprint, arXiv:1804.02767, 2018.

[49] Hengshuang Zhao, Jianping Shi, Xiaojuan Qi, Xiaogang Wang, Jiaya Jia, Pyramid scene parsing network, in: Proceedings of the IEEE Conference on Computer Vision and Pattern Recognition, 2017, pp. 2881–2890.

[50] Olaf Ronneberger, Philipp Fischer, Thomas Brox, U-Net: convolutional networks for biomedical image segmentation, in: International Conference on Medical Image Computing and Computer-Assisted Intervention, Springer, 2015, pp. 234–241.

[51] Simon Jégou, Michal Drozdzal, David Vazquez, Adriana Romero, Yoshua Bengio, The one hundred layers Tiramisu: fully convolutional densenets for semantic segmentation, in: Proceedings of the IEEE Conference on Computer Vision and Pattern Recognition Workshops, 2017, pp. 11–19.

[52] Anisha Pal, Shourya Jaiswal, Swarnendu Ghosh, Nibaran Das, Mita Nasipuri, Segfast: a faster squeezenet based semantic image segmentation technique using depth-wise separable convolutions, in: Proceedings of the 11th Indian Conference on Computer Vision, Graphics and Image Processing, 2018, pp. 1–7.

[53] Swarnendu Ghosh, Anisha Pal, Shourya Jaiswal, KC Santosh, Nibaran Das, Mita Nasipuri, SegFast-V2: semantic image segmentation with less parameters in deep learning for autonomous driving, International Journal of Machine Learning and Cybernetics 10 (11) (2019) 3145–3154.

[54] Forrest N. Iandola, Song Han, Matthew W. Moskewicz, Khalid Ashraf, William J. Dally, Kurt Keutzer, SqueezeNet: AlexNet-level accuracy with 50x fewer parameters and < 0.5 MB model size, preprint, arXiv:1602.07360, 2016.

[55] Arnald Dutta, Bodhisatwa Mandal, Swarnendu Ghosh, Nibaran Das, Using thermal intensities to build conditional random fields for object segmentation at night, in: 2020 4th International Conference on Computational Intelligence and Networks (CINE), IEEE, 2020, pp. 1–6.

[56] Swarnendu Ghosh, Prasenjit Shaw, Nibaran Das, KC Santosh, GSD-Net: compact network for pixel-level graphical symbol detection, in: 13th IAPR International Workshop on Graphics Recognition, GREC@IC-DAR 2019, Sydney, Australia, September 22–25, 2019, IEEE, 2019, pp. 68–73, https://doi.org/10.1109/ICDARW.2019.00017.

[57] Liang-Chieh Chen, George Papandreou, Iasonas Kokkinos, Kevin Murphy, Alan L. Yuille, Deeplab: semantic image segmentation with deep convolutional nets, atrous convolution, and fully connected CRFs, IEEE Transactions on Pattern Analysis and Machine Intelligence 40 (4) (2017) 834–848.

[58] Fisher Yu, Vladlen Koltun, Multi-scale context aggregation by dilated convolutions, preprint, arXiv:1511.07122, 2015.

[59] Krähenbühl Philipp, Vladlen Koltun, Efficient inference in fully connected CRFs with Gaussian edge potentials, in: Advances in Neural Information Processing Systems, 2011, pp. 109–117.

CHAPTER 4

Cytology image analysis

4.1 Background

According to the latest statistics of the WHO [1], cancer is the second deadliest disease in the world. Around 9.6 million deaths or one in six deaths, are accounted in 2018 due to cancer. In general, normal cells are transformed into tumor cells in a multistage process by abnormal growth of cells. Cancer arises from the tumors or precancerous lesion, which generally progresses to a malignant tumor depending upon different factors. Cancer can originate from any organs, such as breast, lung, prostate, colorectal, stomach, cervical, and thyroid. Early detection of cancer is important to reduce the risk of deaths. There are various imaging tools/techniques to detect lumps or masses, such as magnetic resonance imaging (MRI), X-ray (plain film and computed tomography, CT), ultrasound (US), and optical imaging [2]. However, these imaging techniques cannot analyze the images at the cellular level. Therefore different types of microscopic examination of cells/tissues, such as histopathology and cytology, are considered. Among these, cytology is popularly used to detect abnormality in the cell structure at the early stage. In some cases, corelation with other imaging technology may be adapted for appropriate diagnosis.

4.2 Cytology: a brief overview

Cytology is the branch of pathology used for detection of carcinoma by observing the cellular architectures under microscope. Cytology is less invasive in nature when compared to biopsy. Human cells contain nucleus and cytoplasm. The cytoplasm or the cell body acts as a sheath to the nucleus, which contains chromosomes. The genetic material embedded in the chromosome gets mutated during the development of cancer. The changes can be examined through the morphology of nucleus and cytoplasm under microscope. These cells, which are important predictors of premalignant and malignant lesions, are sampled before examination under microscope.

For a benign cell, a well-defined pattern of chromatin in the nucleus with a well-distinguished cytoplasm is observed. The shape of nucleus is elliptical or nearly elliptical with a regular boundary. Malignant cells, on the other hand, are characterized by irregular nuclear texture with multiple nuclei. The nuclei sizes are unusually large (or small) with variations observed. Scanty cytoplasm in malignant cells is also very common. These features are usually considered to classify cytology images.

Deep Learning Models for Medical Imaging
https://doi.org/10.1016/B978-0-12-823504-1.00014-3

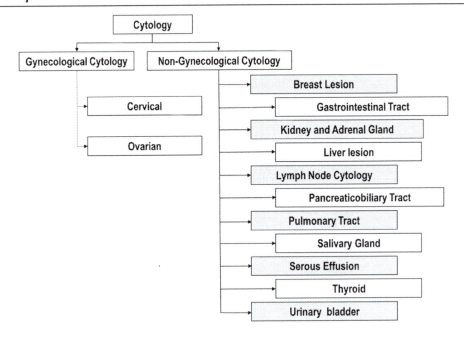

Figure 4.1: A categorization of cytology based on its originating organs.

4.3 Types of cytology

There are several types of cytology based on the originating site of human body. In general, they are categorized into two major groups, gynecological and nongynecological cytology. Cervical and ovarian cytology are normally studied under gynecological cytology. On the other hand, different types of cytology, such as breast, thyroid, respiratory tract, lymph node, liver, kidney and adrenal gland, gastrointestinal tract, pancreaticobiliary, serious effusion, salivary gland, and urinary bladder are categorized under nongynecological cytology. For a better understanding, such divisions are shown in Fig. 4.1. Few images of breast, lung, lymph node, thyroid, and cervical images are shown in Figs. 4.2, 4.3, and 4.4.

4.4 Cytology slide preparation

In cytological test, collection of specimen is the first step where pathologists collect cells from the predestined mass for pathological analysis. Collection techniques are broadly categorized into three approaches: a) aspiration cytology, b) exfoliative cytology, and c) abrasive cytology (see Fig. 4.5).

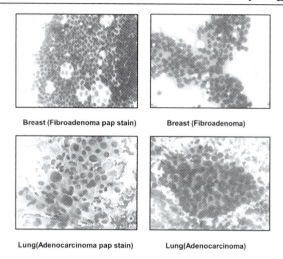

Breast (Fibroadenoma pap stain)   Breast (Fibroadenoma)

Lung(Adenocarcinoma pap stain)   Lung(Adenocarcinoma)

Figure 4.2: Few images of breast and lung cytology with corresponding classes.

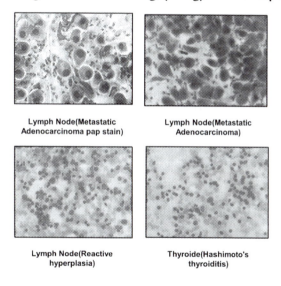

Lymph Node(Metastatic   Lymph Node(Metastatic
Adenocarcinoma pap stain)   Adenocarcinoma)

Lymph Node(Reactive   Thyroide(Hashimoto's
hyperplasia)   thyroiditis)

Figure 4.3: Few images of lymph node and thyroid cytology with corresponding classes.

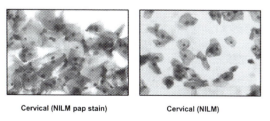

Cervical (NILM pap stain)   Cervical (NILM)

Figure 4.4: Few images of cervical cytology with corresponding classes.

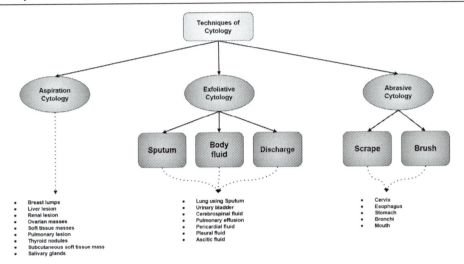

Figure 4.5: Different types of specimen collection techniques and their associated domains in cytology.

4.4.1 Aspiration cytology

In this study, cells are aspirated by using a fine needle of 23–25 gauge from a fluid, cyst, or a palpable mass of clinical suspicion. Prior to injection, the suspected region is swabbed with a cotton soaked in an antiseptic solution. This technique is popularly known as fine needle aspiration (FNA). This is known to be a relatively faster, safer, cheaper, noninvasive, and less painful method compared to surgical biopsy [3]. It is extensively used in the detection and diagnosis of breast lumps, liver lesions, renal lesions, ovarian masses, soft tissue masses, pulmonary lesions, thyroid nodules, subcutaneous soft tissue mass, salivary gland, lymph nodes, and so on [4]. Serious complications are very rare and include redness, soreness, and minor hemorrhage. The first fine-needle aspiration was successfully done at Maimonides Medical Center, United States, in 1981, which paved the way to a near-painless and trauma-free diagnosis process.

4.4.2 Exfoliative cytology

In this study, desquamated cells from the body surfaces or cells are harvested by rubbing or brushing a lesion tissue surface. It consists of three subtypes discussed below.

1) *Body fluid cytology:*
   - Urine;
   - Cerebrospinal fluid (CSF), a fluid that surrounds the brain and spinal cord;

- Pleural fluid (pulmonary effusion), which is an accretion of fluid in the lining of tissues between lungs and the chest cavity;
- Pericardial fluid secreted by the serous layer of the pericardium into the pericardial cavity surrounding the heart; and
- Ascetic fluid (also called ascites or peritoneal fluid) refers to abnormal accumulation fluid in peritoneal or abdominal cavity.

2) *Discharge cytology:*

In this category, cytological examination of breast secretions are carried out to diagnose the disease.

3) *Sputum cytology:*

Sputum is a popular exfoliative cytology, which is usually used for lung disease detection. Sputum (phlegm) is a mixture of mucus and saliva, which consists of exfoliated epithelial cells that line the respiratory tract. Sputum is spontaneous (often aerosol induced) and is coughed up from the lower respiratory tract, that is, from trachea and bronchi. Cytological examination of sputum is done under microscope to detect the presence of malignant cells.

4.4.3 Abrasive cytology

In this procedure the sample is obtained directly from the surface of the region of interest using superficial scraping or brushing of the lesion (artificial mechanical desquamation).

1) *Scrape cytology:*

This technique deals with exfoliation of cells with the help of scrape or brush from the organ or the region being tested. The Pap smear test is a well-known screening test of this kind. Buccal mucosal smear, skin scraping, esophagus, stomach, and so on fall under this category.

2) *Brush cytology:*

It is used to collect cell samples from the gastrointestinal tract, bronchial tree, cervix, and so on.

Preceding to any screening or the diagnostic test, the specimen needs to be prepared. The preparation consists of three steps: a) specimen collection, b) slide preparation, and c) fixation.

4.4.4 Specimen collection

In cytological test, specimen collection is done to collect cells from the predestined mass required for pathological analysis.

4.4.5 Slide preparation

It is one of the important steps for the diagnosis of carcinoma from cytology images, which is equally necessary for both manual and automatic diagnosis systems. After preparing the slide, the fixation is required. Two kinds of slide preparation techniques are normally done in laboratory on the collected specimen and are discussed below.

1) *Conventional preparation:*

   After collection, specimen is expelled into appropriately labeled glass slides with patient's unique identification. The expelled material is spread over several slides in small amounts, rather than deposited in one large pool on a single slide to enhance the probability of error-free interpretation. This eases the process to obtain a thin-layer preparation. Spreading of the material over the slide is usually performed by another sliding glass slide to avoid crushed artifacts and obtain a uniform smear. Large amounts of blood are avoided because when it clots, fibrin trapping in the cells creates large cracks on the slide, which hinders interpretation at cellular level.

2) *Liquid-based preparation:*

   It was introduced initially for cervical smears, but nowadays it is also used for other specimens, including FNA, because this technology has several additional advantages compared to conventional smears. Three preparatory steps: cell dispersion, collection, and transfer prepare such specimen. After collecting the specimen, the aspirate is rinsed directly into a container filled with 20 ml of CytoLyt or CytoRich transport solution, which is an alcohol-based solution. After aspiration, the syringe and needle are thoroughly rinsed into saline or a fixative. If a fresh, nonalcohol-fixed specimen is indicated clinically, then the specimen is put into a balanced electrolyte solution. Two commonly used liquid-based preparation techniques include ThinPrep (TP) (Cytyc Corp, Marlborough, MA) and BD SurePath (SP) (TriPath Imaging Inc., Burlington, NC). Different steps of preparing ThinPrep cytology specimen is shown in Fig. 4.6.

   When compared with conventional preparation, liquid-based preparation offers several advantages:

   • Abundant cellularity in the specimen.
   • Immediate liquid fixation avoids air-drying artifacts.
   • Background contamination like cell clumps, blood, and mucus are absent due to advanced preparatory techniques, which gives a good background clarity.
   • Nuclear and cytoplasmic architecture are well maintained with reduced overlapped nucleus.
   • Normalized specimen.
   • Processing of residual material as a cellblock.

   Despite several advantages, one of the drawbacks of LBP is its reduced background information, which is often required in diagnosing carcinoma.

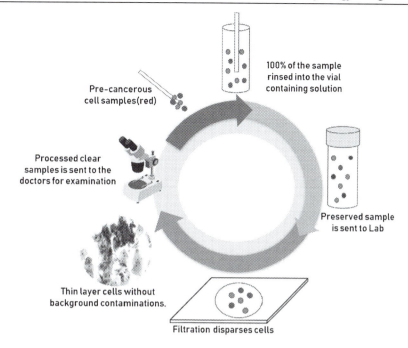

Figure 4.6: Steps to prepare thin prep cytology specimen .

4.4.6 Fixation techniques and staining protocol

Immediate fixation of the collected specimen is crucial, otherwise it produces drying artifact leading to false positives or false negatives cases in medical diagnosis. Two types of fixation techniques are practiced in laboratories, air drying and alcohol drying. Staining is also an essential step, which is usually done after fixation of cytology specimen. Majority of the stains generally fascinate lights and illuminating samples under it. Without staining, it is not possible to identify the selective regions of different tissue samples. The quantity of illumination on a sample or portion of sample depends on the amount and type of stain. However, the same type of stain may vary on multiple factors such as manufacturer of stain, procedure of preservation, and also the condition of specimen before use [5]. Even in case of specimen expertise of cytology, it may vary from one cytotechnologist to another. The intensity can vary depending upon the amount of time it remains under the air drying process.

1) *Air drying:*

   After preparation of the slides, they are immediately fixed by air drying preferably within 5 minutes. Romanowsky stains [6] are usually applied to air-dried smears. Its staining protocol includes May Grunwald Giemsa (MGG) [7], Leishman Giemsa (LG) [8], Diff quick stain, and so on. MGG is the most commonly used staining technique to extract

Table 4.1: Some special stains and applicability.

Special stains	Requirement
Modified Ziehl Neelson [11]	Acid fast bacilli smear and culture
Gram staining [12]	Bacteria
Mucicarmine [13]	Mucins
PAS (Periodic Acid-Schif) [14]	Glycogen, Fungal wall, and Lipofuscin
Oil red O [15]	Lipids
Perl's Prussian blue [16]	Iron
Modified Fouchet's test [17]	Bilirubin

cellular morphology and cytoplasm details from air-dried smears. Tubercle bacilli, Actinomyces, some fungal elements appear red, and background appears pale blue in color on application of this particular stain.

2) *Alcohol fixation:*

Alcohol or wet fixation is achieved either by using a spray fixative or by dipping the slides in 95% ethyl alcohol. Papanicolaou stain [9] is normally preferred for the staining of alcohol-fixed slides. Squamous differentiation can be best appreciated by Papanicolau stain. The staining protocol includes Papanicolaou-EA-50 to stain critical portions of nucleus and cytoplasm. Harris' hematoxylin [10] is a combination of OG6 (Orange G) and EA50 (Eosin Azure). OG6 is a Pap reagent for counter staining exfoliative cytology samples like vaginal, cervical, prostatic smears, and so on. After application of the stain the nucleus appears blue/black. The cytoplasm for keratinizing cells appears pink/orange and blue/green in color for nonkeratinizing squamous cells. Some special stains are mentioned in Table 4.1.

4.5 Cytological process and digitization

Appropriate slides of the specimen are prepared maintaining organ-specific protocol and then undergone for screening or a diagnostic test. In general, this process is done manually by expert cytotechnologist. After appropriate examination of the slide under microscope, the final verdict is produced by the doctor/medical experts about the specimen of the slides. For this, developing automation systems by taking image processing tools (deep learning) is interesting [18]. Various automation techniques [19–28] were applied for primary screening of slides, where experts can target only on specific areas of slides. However, most of them are not commercially available [29,30]. We provide few key survey papers that extended discussion on the progress of cytology automation techniques [31–36].

Before introducing an automated approach, visual/manual interpretation under microscope was practiced for cytological image analysis. The result is assessed based on the examination of cells under microscope by skilled practitioners, which is a dearth as of now. To reduce human intervention, automated tools are needed. The major objective of computer-assisted diagnostic system (automated tools) is reducing the time taken to perform the tests and complete the process of report generation. There are several other factors, such as reducing the workload of cytotechnologists, reducing human-induced errors, allowing batch processing, which put steps forward toward automation. Automated systems can be further categorized into two sections.

- It can act as prescreening system to distinguish between normal and abnormal specimens. Such systems generally exhibit high false-positive cases. Thus, in another sense, it can act as an adjunct to the cytotechnologists by eliminating the need of evaluating normal specimens, which saves time and energy of the doctors.
- Another way to implement an automated system is to run the system in a parallel fashion to the present manual screening procedure. Thus, the diagnosis process becomes bidirected such that there are less chances of errors at the specimen level, and false-negative cases are reduced.

Despite limited success achieved so far with the existing systems, there were constant efforts to upgrade and design automated screening systems on a large scale. There were a handful of designs developed during the 1980s like BioPEPR [37], FAZYTAN [38], CERVISCAN [39], LEYTAS [40], and so on. In cytology laboratories, there are three major sections as discussed below, where automations are extremely pertinent, and devices are currently accessible.

1) *Specimen collection and preparation devices:*
   Recently, two automated systems have got FDA (Food and Drug Administration) approval for this purpose, namely, ThinPrep Processor and the AutoCyte Prep. ThinPrep processor 5000 uses thin prep technology for cell dispersion, collection, and transfer, which can process approximately 35 slides per hour. AutoCyte prep also uses liquid-based preparations. However, the preparation of monolayer slides in two systems are outright different.
2) *Manual screening adjunctive devices:*
   These devices reduce examining whole slides. Thus examining the whole slide is not required. Also, screening machines require high degree of automation with high-precision parts and delicate optics. Some of the computerized microscopes, such as CompuCyte's M Pathfinder and Accumed International's AcCell 2000, widely accepted by FDA approved system, can help to mark abnormal cells.
3) *Automated screening devices:*
   To automate the process, the interpretation of cytology smears, auto-Pap screener system, an existing system is designed to present a portion of slide that is adequate for analysis by cytotechnologist, thus trimming their workload to go through whole specimen.

4.6 Cervical cell cytology

According to the latest WHO report [41], cervical cancer is now the fourth most frequent cancer in women. It originates from woman's cervix and later invades other parts of the body. In earlier stages, it is very hard to identify any symptom. In advanced stage, symptoms like abnormal vaginal bleeding, increased vaginal discharge, bleeding after going through menopause, abdominal pain, and so on are observed. The cause of cervical cancer is human papilloma virus (HPV) infection that causes cervical dysplasia, or abnormal growth of cervical cells. There are mainly four types of cervical cancer.

1) *Squamous cell carcinomas:*
   It is the most common form of malignant tumor of cervix and accounts for nearly 85% of the overall cervical cancer in women of age between 40 and 55 years. These cells line the outer surface of the cervix and are thin- and flat-shaped.
2) *Adenocarcinomas:*
   It originates in the glandular cells that line the upper area of cervix and accounts for 10% of the overall cases of cervical cancer. The mean age of patients is 55 years.
3) *Adenosquamous carcinomas:*
   As the name implies, it consists of both the squamous and glandular cells and accounts for nearly 2–3% of cervical cancers.
4) *Small cell carcinomas:*
   Generally, very aggressive in nature and rarely found (2–3%), which correspond to stage IV of the cancer. Its cytomorphology exhibits a nesting pattern and is often arranged in sheets.

4.6.1 Modalities of cervical specimen collection

Cervical smears are obtained using a spatula and brush and categorized under brush cytology. The samples are exfoliated from ectocervix and endocervix by rotating a plastic spatula in 360 degrees. The sample is smeared on the slide, which is spray-fixed immediately to avoid air-drying artifact. This technique was developed George Papanicolaou and hence known as the Papanicolaou test or Pap smear test.

4.6.2 Characteristics of cytomorphology of malignant cells

Malignant cells of cervix differ significantly from benign cells in shape, size, and texture. Generally, malignant cells are found in clusters of small cells with scant cytoplasm. Nuclear membrane irregularity is also commonly observed in malignant cells. These characteristics are important in classifying the specimens into benign and malignant.

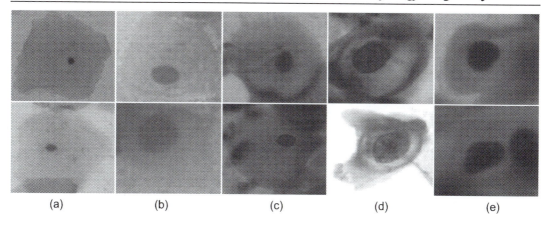

(a)　　　　(b)　　　　(c)　　　　(d)　　　　(e)

Figure 4.7: Few images of a cell from SipakMed dataset for different categories:
a) superficial-intermediate cell, b) parabasal cell, c) metaplastic cell, d) koilocytotic cell, and
e) dyskeratotic cell.

4.7 Experiments

In this section, we discuss different datasets with the characteristics of the datasets. Besides, in subsequent section, we discuss three different protocols involved in the experiment using deep learning module selecting a particular dataset.

4.7.1 Dataset

In cytology, the number of publicly available datasets are comparatively lower than the other medical fields [42], such as histopathology, skin disease, hematology, ultrasonography, and X-rays. Among different types cytology, only cervical cytology has few numbers of publicly available datasets such as a) Herlev [43], b) SipakMed [44], c) Mendeley LBP Cytology [45], d) Cervix 93 [46], and e) ISBI-2014,2015 overlapping cytology image dataset. Among them, (a)–(c) are commonly used for classification, and (a), (d), and (e) are used for segmentation task. Among all the datasets, we have selected SipakMed to evaluate the performance of different deep learning models (see Figs. 4.7 and 4.8). As shown in Table 4.2, SipakMed consists of both single cell and whole slide and has five different categories: a) dyskeratotic, b) koilocytotic, c) metaplastic, d) parabasal, and e) superficial-intermediate. Among the five classes, 1–2 classes belong to the abnormal cervical cells, and 4–5 classes represent normal cervical cells, and 3 represents the benign cells. The dataset consists of 4049 numbers of single cells collected from 996 slides. The classwise data distributions are described in Table 4.3. In this chapter, we have distributed data into 3:1:1 ratio for training, validation, and testing, maintaining a class-specific distribution for our experiment.

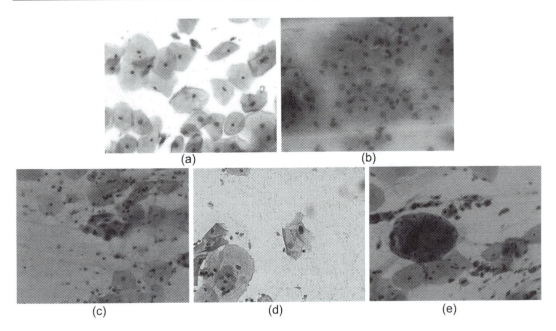

Figure 4.8: Few images of "whole slide" from SipakMed dataset for different categories:
a) superficial-intermediate cell, b) parabasal cell, c) metaplastic cell, d) koilocytotic cell, and
e) dyskeratotic cell.

Table 4.2:   List of publicly available datasets in cytology domain.

Dataset	Slide types	# of classes	# of samples	Types of task
Herlev	Single cell	7	917	Classification/ Segmentation
SIPaKMeD	Single cell, whole slide	5	4049	Classification
Mendeley LBC	Whole slide	4	963	Classification
Cervix93	Whole slide	3	93	Classification/ Segmentation
ISBI 2014/2015	Whole slide	–	17	Segmentation

Table 4.3:   SIPaKMeD Pap smear dataset distribution.

Class	Category	Cell type	# of cells	Total
1	Normal	Superficial-Intermediate	831	Normal = 1618
2	Normal	Parabasal	787	
3	Abnormal	Koilocytotic	825	Abnormal = 1638
4	Abnormal	Dyskeratotic	813	
5	Benign	Metaplastic	793	Benign = 793

4.7.2 Experimental setup and protocols

In this section, we demonstrate how to design a deep convolutional network to classify cytology images on single cell and cluster of cells or whole slide. To do that, three popular deep learning modules, ResNet-34, InceptionNet-V3, and DenseNet-161 are used. The basic architectures of the networks have already been described in the previous chapters. We discuss their usages changing different parameters, that is, with/without pretrained network, using different activation functions, and with or without data augmentation. Moreover, we also demonstrate an improved performance of the system using the ensemble of networks. Based on these, we categorized our experiments into three protocols:

1) Evaluating the performance of deep learning models with or without transfer learning;
2) Boosting the performance using data augmentation; and
3) Boosting the performance using the ensemble of classifiers.

4.7.2.1 Transfer learning: a quick overview

Transfer learning is a popular concept in the domain of deep learning, where a model is developed for a machine learning task and reused to solve another task. It helps quickly tune the parameters for the second task and improve generalization. Thus it boosts the performance of the second task in terms of accuracy and time complexity. Theoretically, transfer learning can be used for multiple tasks, but proximity among two tasks normally enhances the performance of the second model. For example, ImageNet dataset consists of 1000 classes for natural object detection. The trained model can be used for other types of object detection that has some close symmetry with the others. The performance may not be improved significantly if the close proximity does not exist. In worst cases the performance of the transferred domain may decrease, which is referred to as a negative transfer. The transfer learning is normally categorized into inductive, transductive, and unsupervised depending upon the setting between the source and target domains. An overview of different settings with source domain relationship is given in Table 4.4. Different approaches are used for each transfer learning settings. Thus transfer learning is also categorized into four different types: a) instance transfer, b) feature-representation transfer, c) parameter transfer, and d) relational-knowledge transfer based on their approaches [47].

1) *Instance transfer:*
   In this category, target domain uses reweight or selects instances of source domain to reduce the discrepancy between source and target domains.
2) *Feature-representation transfer:*
   The target domain uses "good" feature representations, which are identified from the source domain to minimize the error of classification and regression models

Table 4.4: Different settings of transfer learning for source/domain labels.

Transfer learning setting	Source domain labels	Target domain labels	Tasks
Inductive transfer learning	Available	Available	Classification/Regression
Transductive transfer learning	Available	Unavailable	Classification/Regression
Unsupervised transfer learning	Unavailable	Unavailable	Clustering/Dimensionality reduction

3) *Parameter transfer:*
   In this category, shared parameters or priors between the source and target domain models are identified to improve performance.
4) *Relational-knowledge transfer:*
   Based on the relational knowledge between the source and target domains, a mapping is developed. Both domains should be in relational knowledge transfer domains where i.i.d. assumption is not considered strictly.

The detailed descriptions of the transfer learning are not discussed in this book. In this chapter, we empirically study the concept of transfer learning on the SIPAKmed, a free standard cervical cytology dataset. As described previously, the dataset consists of the whole slide and a single cell. We have experimented individually for both types of datasets with or without transfer learning separately.

For a small dataset, deep learning performance may not give the desired result due to lack of variations in training samples. To mitigate the issue, researchers used different types of data augmentation, such as rotation, noise, and flipping [48]. Inclusion of augmented multiple samples may also help the network prevent from overfitting of training data. However, it does not ensure the performance boosting in all the cases. To overcome such issues, researchers developed several synthetic data-generation techniques using the adversarial neural network [49] to augment the data. Researchers used other methods like different decision fusion techniques, such as majority voting and average probability, to improve the performance of individual network decision.

4.7.3 Results and discussion

4.7.3.1 Results with or without using transfer learning

In this chapter, we experiment with three popular deep learning networks: ResNet-34, InceptionNet-V3, and DenseNet-161 on Sipakmed dataset. The dataset consists of whole slide images and single-cell images. As mentioned earlier, train, validation, and test set on

Table 4.5: **Number of parameters used in different architectures.**

Architecture	# of layers	Filter layers conv. $n \times n$	Filter sizes layers	Pooling layers	Classification (conv. 1D vector)	Total # of parameters
ResNet34	36	33	(3×3), (7×7)	2	1	21,287,237
Inception-v3	48	98	(1×1), (3×3), (5×5), (1×7), (7×1)	14	1	21,795,813
DenseNet161	161	160	(1×1), (3×3)	1	0	21,800,237

Sipakmed dataset are distributed into 3:1:1 ratio for both cases. Therefore, for the whole slide images, train, validation, and test datasets consist of 581, 189, 196 samples, respectively, whereas 2431, 805, and 813 samples are there in the train, validation, and test set for single-cell dataset, respectively. As discussed in the previous chapter, there exist different types of optimizers, such as Tanh, Adam, RmsProp, and SGD. We have empirically observed the performance of the three popular optimizers along with variations in activation functions. In the literature, there exist several activation functions: linear sigmoid, Tanh, ReLU, Leaky ReLU, parameterized ReLU, exponential linear unit, Softmax, Swish function, and MISH, which are used in the convolutional neural networks. Among those, we have selected Tanh, ReLU, and MISH for the present work. We have experimented with these three popular optimization techniques with three different activation functions for the three CNN architectures on the whole slide images and single-cell images separately. The parameters required for each architecture for the present work are summarized in Table 4.5.

The results obtained without or with transfer learning are reported in Tables 4.6 and 4.7. From them we observe that SGDS with MISH function give maximum recognition accuracies on the test sets of both datasets without transfer learning and on the test set of single-slide image dataset with transfer learning. For transfer learning-based cases, ResNet-34 having Adam optimizer with ReLu gave maximum accuracies, but the performance is comparable with SGDS with MISH activation function. For InceptionNet-V3, SGDS optimizer gave the best results for whole slide and single-cell image datasets with or without using the pretrained network of transfer learning. ReLU-based activation function gave the best results for pretrained networks, whereas MISH activation gave better results for the network trained from the beginning. The DenseNet-161 having Adam with ReLu gave better results for the pretrained network in both cases of whole slides and single cells and for the network training from the beginning for single cells. For whole slide images, MISH function gave the best results. From Table 4.5 we see that DenseNet-161 takes a lower number of parameters compared to other networks, but the performance is better than in other networks for both cases.

Table 4.6:   Results of ResNet-34 using transfer learning.

Optimizer	Activation function	Accuracy (cellwise)	Accuracy (whole slide)
ADAM	TanH	84.25	81.63
	ReLU	91.27	91.33
	MISH	90.90	77.04
RMSprop	TanH	84.13	63.26
	ReLU	94.34	84.69
	MISH	89.91	71.94
SGDS	TanH	78.84	85.70
	ReLU	93.60	85.20
	MISH	94.34	90.82

Table 4.7:   Results of ResNet-34 without transfer learning.

Optimizer	Activation function	Accuracy (cellwise)	Accuracy (whole slide)
ADAM	TanH	85.49	43.88
	ReLU	90.6	75
	MISH	89.54	76.02
RMSprop	TanH	84.75	57.14
	ReLU	85.85	66.83
	MISH	85.98	65.31
SGDS	TanH	90.77	83.67
	ReLU	88.43	73.46
	MISH	94.83	86.73

Table 4.8:   Results of InceptionNet-V3 using transfer learning.

Optimizer	Activation function	Accuracy (cellwise)	Accuracy (whole slide)
ADAM	TanH	86.70	78.30
	ReLU	92.29	88.89
	MISH	80.01	88.36
RMSprop	TanH	85.09	72.49
	ReLU	86.33	80.95
	MISH	81.14	63.492
SGDS	TanH	90.43	88.89
	ReLU	94.28	91.00
	MISH	92.12	85.18

From Tables 4.6, 4.7, 4.8, 4.9, 4.10, and 4.11 we can observe that SGDS with MISH function provided better results in most cases compared to the combination of MISH function with other optimizers for the dataset. Combination of ADAM+RELU gave better results than the other activation functions combined with Adam optimizer. For RMSProp, ReLU provided

Table 4.9: Results of InceptionNet-V3 without transfer learning.

Optimizer	Activation function	Accuracy (cellwise)	Accuracy (whole slide)
ADAM	TanH	88.89	86.00
	ReLU	90.77	80.61
	MISH	90.6	83.16
RMSprop	TanH	84.09	84.00
	ReLU	91.26	79.08
	MISH	90.89	85.2
SGDS	TanH	89.69	90.00
	ReLU	91.88	87.25
	MISH	95.45	87.75

Table 4.10: Results of DenseNet-161 using transfer learning.

Optimizer	Activation function	Accuracy (cellwise)	Accuracy (whole slide)
ADAM	TanH	92.4	81.5
	ReLU	97.54	91.5
	MISH	95.73	87.5
RMSprop	TanH	90.8	82
	ReLU	96.2	91
	MISH	95.6	90
SGDS	TanH	92.4	84.33
	ReLU	97.44	89.4
	MISH	93.7	82

Table 4.11: Results of DenseNet-161 without transfer learning.

Optimizer	Activation function	Accuracy (cellwise)	Accuracy (whole slide)
ADAM	TanH	87.08	79.08
	ReLU	95.7	84.2
	MISH	86.96	81.63
RMSprop	TanH	71.22	62.76
	ReLU	94.34	70.4
	MISH	70.6	74.49
SGDS	TanH	92.13	83.16
	ReLU	86.96	75.51
	MISH	95.57	87.76

better results in most cases. Moreover, we can observe that transfer learning provided better results than training the model from scratches. However, the source and target domain image characteristics are entirely different in these cases. We have used a pretrained network of ImageNet having 1000 output classes of natural scene objects compared to only five classes in

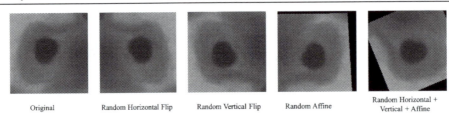

| | | | | Random Horizontal + |
| Original | Random Horizontal Flip | Random Vertical Flip | Random Affine | Vertical + Affine |

Figure 4.9: Few images after applying different augmentations on a cell image.

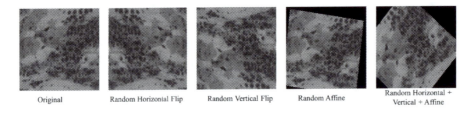

| | | | | Random Horizontal + |
| Original | Random Horizontal Flip | Random Vertical Flip | Random Affine | Vertical + Affine |

Figure 4.10: Few images after applying different augmentations on a cell image.

the present work. During transfer learning, we have freezed first few layers to get lower-level features from the pretrained network. The exact number of layers is decided empirically on network-to-network basis.

4.7.3.2 Results with data augmentation

The performance of deep learning techniques highly depends on the variations of data distributions. The network generally overfitted with the lower number of data. To reduce the overfitting, there are several methods, such as dropout, normalization, and data augmentation used frequently by the researchers. Introduction of traditional data augmentation techniques does not guarantee an improvement of the performance [48,49]. To overcome the issues, a new branch of research for the generation of synthetic data has evolved using generative adversarial neural network [49]. In this study, we do not discuss the details of those techniques, but rather focus on traditional data augmentation techniques. Therefore we consider horizontal and vertical flips, affine transform, and combination of these transformations. Such transformations and flipping are done randomly. We use random affine transformation with the following parameters: a) rotation (-180 deg to 180 deg); b) translation by a factor of 0.1 times image height and width; c) scale by a factor of 0.9 times image height and 1.1 time image width; d) shear angle (-5 degree to 5 degree); and e) normalization with mean $= [0.485, 0.456, 0.406]$ and standard deviation $= [0.229, 0.224, 0.225]$. Figs. 4.9 and 4.10 show the examples of such augmentations. Instead of rerunning all the experiments of different networks with data augmentation, we used the best models from the set, that is, DenseNet-161 with ADAM optimizer consisting of ReLU activation function with transfer learning is used

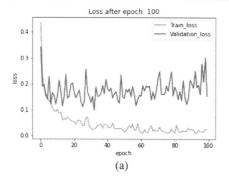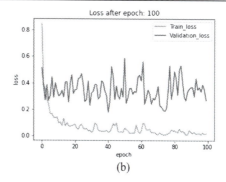

(a) (b)

Figure 4.11: Train and validation loss curves for the best models using DenseNet-161 on a) cell dataset and b) whole slide dataset.

Class#	1	2	3	4	5
1	161	2	0	0	0
2	2	159	5	0	0
3	1	2	156	0	0
4	0	0	0	158	0
5	0	0	2	0	165

(a)

Class#	1	2	3	4	5
1	41	3	1	0	0
2	3	41	1	0	3
3	2	2	51	0	0
4	0	0	0	22	0
5	0	1	0	0	25

(b)

Figure 4.12: Confusion matrix achieved for the best models using DenseNet-161 on a) cell dataset and b) whole slide dataset.

for both single-cell and whole slide datasets. A glimpse of train and validation loss for the network up to 110 epochs is shown in Fig. 4.11. Using this, we have obtained maximum accuracies of 97.55 and 92.63% on test datasets of single-cell and whole slide images. The confusion matrices on test datasets for single-cell and whole slide images are shown in Fig. 4.12. The achieved accuracies are better than those without data augmentation, which indicate the significance of data augmentation techniques of the present work. Some sample images, which are not classified properly, are shown in Figs. 4.13 and 4.14 for single-cell and whole ` slide test image datasets, respectively.

4.7.3.3 Results using ensemble of classifiers

To enhance performance, researchers use an ensemble of classifiers. Generally, the ensemble of classifiers provides more accurate results than the performance of individual classifiers. Therefore researchers heavily rely on the ensemble of classifiers during the development of an accurate system. Several variations of ensembling techniques exist in the literature [50]. In this study, we evaluated different ensembling techniques on the performance of the best models from the architectures of ResNet-34, InceptionNet-V3, and DenseNet-161 (see

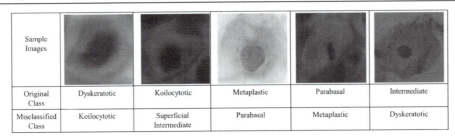

Sample Images					
Original Class	Dyskeratotic	Koilocytotic	Metaplastic	Parabasal	Intermediate
Misclassified Class	Koilocytotic	Superficial Intermediate	Parabasal	Metaplastic	Dyskeratotic

Figure 4.13: Few missclassified cell images along with their original and classified classes.

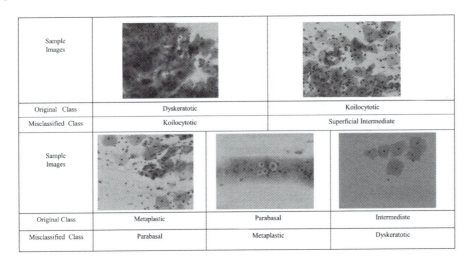

Sample Images		
Original Class	Dyskeratotic	Koilocytotic
Misclassified Class	Koilocytotic	Superficial Intermediate
Sample Images		
Original Class	Metaplastic	Parabasal	Intermediate
Misclassified Class	Parabasal	Metaplastic	Dyskeratotic

Figure 4.14: Few missclassified whole slide images along with their original and classified class.

Table 4.12). During combination, we used all three networks and their possible pairs. The mathematics of ensembling techniques is given below.

Let x, C, N be the testing data, total number of classifiers used for ensembling techniques, and the total number of output classes, respectively. Let L_i be the ith class (where $i = 1, \ldots N$), and let $P_k(\frac{x}{L_i})$ be the probability distribution value of testing data x of L_i class label with respect to the kth classifier.

1) *Average probability:*
   The average probability value for class L_i is $\frac{1}{C} \sum_{k=1}^{C} P_k(\frac{x}{L_i}) = P_{\text{Avg}}(\frac{x}{L_i})$ (let us assume). Therefore the predicted class for the test data x is $\text{argmax}_{L_i} \{ P_{\text{Avg}}(\frac{x}{L_i}) \}_{i=1}^{N}$.

2) *Min rule:*
   The min probability value for class L_i is $\min\{ P_k(\frac{x}{L_i}) \}_{k=1}^{C} = P_{\text{Min}}(\frac{x}{L_i})$. Therefore the predicted class for the test data x is $\text{argmax}_{L_i} \{ P_{\text{Min}}(\frac{x}{L_i}) \}_{i=1}^{N}$.

Table 4.12: Different statistics for the best model (using different architectures) on single-cell and whole slide datasets.

Architecture	Class	Cell dataset			Whole slide dataset		
		Recall	Precision	F-score	Recall	Precision	F-score
ResNet-34	Class #1	0.9755	0.9298	0.9521	0.9333	0.8936	0.9130
	Class #2	0.8855	0.9074	0.8963	0.8958	0.8776	0.8866
	Class #3	0.8994	0.9408	0.9196	0.8909	0.9245	0.9074
	Class #4	1.0000	0.9814	0.9906	1.0000	1.0000	1.0000
	Class #5	0.9820	0.9820	0.9820	0.8846	0.9200	0.9020
	Average	0.9485	0.9483	0.9481	0.9209	0.9231	0.9218
InceptionNet-V3	Class #1	0.9755	0.9755	0.9755	0.9333	0.8750	0.9032
	Class #2	0.8916	0.8970	0.8943	0.8125	0.8298	0.8211
	Class #3	0.9308	0.9136	0.9221	0.8364	0.9388	0.8846
	Class #4	0.9937	0.9874	0.9905	0.9546	0.9546	0.9546
	Class #5	0.9820	1.0000	0.9909	0.9615	0.8333	0.8929
	Average	0.9547	0.9547	0.9547	0.8997	0.8863	0.8913
DenseNet-161	Class #1	0.9877	0.9758	0.9817	0.9333	0.8936	0.9130
	Class #2	0.9217	0.9745	0.9474	0.8750	0.9130	0.8936
	Class #3	0.9874	0.9401	0.9632	0.8909	0.9423	0.9159
	Class #4	1.0000	1.0000	1.0000	0.9545	1.0000	0.9767
	Class #5	0.9940	1.0000	0.9970	1.0000	0.8667	0.9286
	Average	0.9782	0.9781	0.9779	0.9308	0.9231	0.9256

3) *Max rule:*

The max probability value for class L_i is $\max\{P_k(\frac{x}{L_i})\}_{k=1}^{C} = P_{\text{Max}}(\frac{x}{L_i})$. Therefore the predicted class for the test data x is $\text{argmax}_{L_i}\{P_{\text{Max}}(\frac{x}{L_i})\}_{i=1}^{N}$.

4) *Majority voting rule:*

We evaluate the predicted class for each kth classifier of the test data x. Let L_i^k be the predicted class for test data x with respect to the kth classifier: $L_i^k \leftarrow \text{argmax}_{L_i}\{P_k(\frac{x}{L_i})\}_{i=1}^{N}$. Therefore the predicted class for the test data x is $\text{Mode}_{L_i}\{L_i^k\}_{k=1}^{C}$.

The performances on the test dataset of SipakMeddataset using a) majority voting, b) average probability, c) min rule, and d) max rule are shown in Table 4.13. In the table the maximum accuracy of 97.66% was achieved using the combination of InceptionNet-V3 and DenseNet-161, and the min rule ensemble technique was considered. Using the min rule ensemble technique, the maximum accuracy of 92.86 was reported for two combinations: a) ResNet-34, InceptionNet-V3, and DenseNet-161 and b) ReseNet-34 and DenseNet-161 on the test dataset of whole slide images. We observed that DenseNet-161 was involved for all the highest cases and thus ensures its superiority on SipakMed dataset.

Table 4.13: Results obtained using different ensembling techniques on SipakMed dataset.

CNN combinations	Data type	Average probability	Min rule	Max rule	Majority voting
ResNet-34 + InseptionNetV3 + DenseNet-161	Cell	96.56	96.68	97.17	96.92
	Slide	92.35	92.86	91.84	92.86
ResNet-34 + InceptionNetV3	Cell	0.9582	0.9606	0.9557	–
	Slide	0.8827	0.9082	0.8827	–
ResNet-34 + DenseNet-161	Cell	0.9705	0.9705	0.9717	–
	Slide	0.9235	0.9286	0.9184	–
InceptionNet-V3 + DenseNet-161	Cell	0.9729	0.9692	0.9766	–
	Slide	0.9184	0.9184	0.9184	–

4.7.4 Summary

On the whole, we have discussed the performance of three popular deep learning architectures, ResNet-34, InceptionNet-V3, and DenseNet-161 on SipakMed dataset, a cervical cytology dataset having whole slide and single-slide images distributed in five classes.

To understand the effect of different optimization techniques, we have employed three different popular optimizers, ADAM, RmsProp, and SGDs varying three activation functions, and reported their results with or without using the transfer learning modules. We have also demonstrated that data augmentation may or may not improve the performance significantly based on the experiment based on the best model. We have also illustrated the implementations of different classifier ensembling techniques and observed better understanding than the individual classifier.

We empirically observed that transfer learning generally provides better results than training the network from scratch. The performance can be further improved using data augmentation or classifier combination.

References

[1] W.H.O. Cancer, https://www.who.int/news-room/fact-sheets/detail/cancer, Sep 2018.

[2] John V. Frangioni, New technologies for human cancer imaging, Journal of Clinical Oncology 26 (24) (Aug 2008) 4012–4021, https://doi.org/10.1200/jco.2007.14.3065.

[3] Henryk A. Domanski, Fine-needle aspiration cytology of soft tissue lesions: diagnostic challenges, Diagnostic Cytopathology (ISSN 8755-1039) 35 (12) (2007) 768–773, https://doi.org/10.1002/dc.20765.

[4] P. Lopes Cardozo, The significance of fine needle aspiration cytology for the diagnosis and treatment of malignant lymphomas, Folia Haematologica (Leipzig, Germany: 1928) (ISSN 0323-4347) 107 (4) (1980) 601–620 (Print).

[5] M. Macenko, M. Niethammer, J.S. Marron, D. Borland, J.T. Woosley, Xiaojun Guan, C. Schmitt, N.E. Thomas, A method for normalizing histology slides for quantitative analysis, in: 2009 IEEE International Symposium on Biomedical Imaging: From Nano to Macro, June 2009, pp. 1107–1110.

[6] D.H. Wittekind, On the nature of Romanowsky–Giemasa staining and its significance for cytochemistry and histochemistry: an overall view, The Histochemical Journal 15 (10) (1983) 1029–1047.

[7] Paul Lopes Cardozo, Clinical Cytology: Using the May–Grünwald–Giemsa Stained Smear. 2. Atlas, Stafleu, 1954.

[8] Shilpa Manigatta Doddagowda, Hemalatha Anantharamaiah Shashidhar, Chinaiah Subramanyam Babu Rajendra Prasad, Leishman–Giemsa cocktail – is it an effective stain for air dried cytology smears, Journal of Clinical and Diagnostic Research: JCDR 11 (3) (2017) EC16.

[9] Todd K. Berkan, Jay E. Reeder, Peter A. Lopez Jr., Kevin M. Gorman, Leon L. Wheeless Jr., A protocol for Papanicolaou staining of cytologic specimens following flow analysis, Cytometry: The Journal of the International Society for Analytical Cytology 7 (1) (1986) 101–103.

[10] Yawu Li, Ning Li, Xiang Yu, Kai Huang, Ting Zheng, Xiaofeng Cheng, Shaoqun Zeng, Xiuli Liu, Hematoxylin and eosin staining of intact tissues via delipidation and ultrasound, Scientific Reports 8 (1) (2018) 12259.

[11] Janet L. Allen, A modified Ziehl-Neelsen stain for mycobacteria, Medical Laboratory Sciences 49 (2) (1992) 99–102.

[12] T. Gregersen, Rapid method for distinction of gram-negative from gram-positive bacteria, European Journal of Applied Microbiology and Biotechnology 5 (2) (1978) 123–127.

[13] James H. Cherry, Ralph K. Ghormley, A histopathological study of the synovial membrane with mucicarmine staining, JBJS: The Journal of Bone & Joint Surgery 20 (1) (1938) 48–56.

[14] M.L. Warnock, A. Stoloff, A. Thor, Differentiation of adenocarcinoma of the lung from mesothelioma. Periodic acid-Schiff, monoclonal antibodies B72. 3, and Leu M1, The American Journal of Pathology 133 (1) (1988) 30.

[15] J.L. Ramirez-Zacarias, F. Castro-Munozledo, W. Kuri-Harcuch, Quantitation of adipose conversion and triglycerides by staining intracytoplasmic lipids with oil red O, Histochemistry 97 (6) (1992) 493–497.

[16] A. Peter Hall, Wendy Davies, Katie Stamp, Isabel Clamp, Alison Bigley, Comparison of computerized image analysis with traditional semiquantitative scoring of Perls' Prussian Blue stained hepatic iron deposition, Toxicologic Pathology 41 (7) (2013) 992–1000.

[17] Daphne Bryant, F.V. Flynn, An assessment of new tests for detecting bilirubin in urine, Journal of Clinical Pathology 8 (2) (1955) 163.

[18] Shyamali Mitra, Nibaran Das, Soumyajyoti Dey, Sukanta Chakrabarty, Mita Nasipuri, Mrinal Kanti Naskar, Cytology image analysis techniques towards automation: systematically revisited, 2020.

[19] W.N. Street, Xcyt: a system for remote cytological diagnosis and prognosis of breast cancer, in: Artificial Intelligence Techniques in Breast Cancer Diagnosis and Prognosis, in: Series in Machine Perception and Artificial Intelligence, vol. 39, World Scientific Publishing Co., Aug 2000, pp. 297–326.

[20] Jian Yang, Yikai Zhou, Detection of DNA aneuploidy in exfoliated airway epithelia cells of sputum specimens by the automated image cytometry and its clinical value in the identification of lung cancer, Journal of Huazhong University of Science and Technology. Medical sciences = Hua zhong ke ji da xue xue bao. Yi xue Ying De wen ban = Huazhong keji daxue xuebao. Yixue Yingdewen ban 24 (4) (2004) 407–410.

[21] Anne E. Carpenter, Thouis R. Jones, Michael R. Lamprecht, Colin Clarke, In Han Kang, Ola Friman, David A. Guertin, Joo Han Chang, Robert A. Lindquist, Jason Moffat, Polina Golland, David M. Sabatini, CellProfiler: image analysis software for identifying and quantifying cell phenotypes, Genome Biology (ISSN 1474-760X) 7 (10) (Oct 2006) 1–11, https://doi.org/10.1186/gb-2006-7-10-r100.

[22] Roger A. Kemp, Daniel M. Reinders, Bojana Turic, Detection of lung cancer by automated sputum cytometry, Journal of Thoracic Oncology 2 (11) (2007) 993–1000.

[23] D.C. Wilbur, Digital cytology: current state of the art and prospects for the future, Acta Cytologica (ISSN 0001-5547) 55 (3) (2011) 227–238, https://www.karger.com/DOI/10.1159/000324734.

[24] Arnab Ghosh, Dilasma Ghartimagar, Manish Kiran Shrestha, P.K. Tiwari, Raghavan Narasimhan, O.P. Talwar, Value of image-guided fine-needle aspiration cytology – a study of 500 cases, Diagnostic Cytopathology (ISSN 8755-1039) 41 (12) (2013) 1052–1062, https://doi.org/10.1002/dc.22922.

[25] Y.M. George, H.H. Zayed, M.I. Roushdy, B.M. Elbagoury, Remote computer-aided breast cancer detection and diagnosis system based on cytological images, IEEE Systems Journal (ISSN 1932-8184) 8 (3) (2014) 949–964, https://doi.org/10.1109/JSYST.2013.2279415.

[26] Geert Litjens, Thijs Kooi, Babak Ehteshami Bejnordi, Arnaud Arindra Adiyoso Setio, Francesco Ciompi, Mohsen Ghafoorian, Jeroen A.W.M. van der Laak, Bram van Ginneken, Clara I. Sánchez, A survey on deep learning in medical image analysis, Medical Image Analysis (ISSN 1361-8423) 42 (12) (2017) 60–88, https://doi.org/10.1016/j.media.2017.07.005.

[27] Ling Zhang, Le Lu, Isabella Nogues, Ronald M. Summers, Shaoxiong Liu, Jianhua Yao, DeepPap: deep convolutional networks for cervical cell classification, IEEE Journal of Biomedical and Health Informatics (ISSN 2168-2194) 21 (6) (2017) 1633–1643, https://doi.org/10.1109/JBHI.2017.2705583.

[28] Y. Chen, P. Huang, K. Lin, H. Lin, L. Wang, C. Cheng, T. Chen, Y. Chan, J.Y. Chiang, Semi-automatic segmentation and classification of Pap smear cells, IEEE Journal of Biomedical and Health Informatics 18 (1) (2014) 94–108.

[29] Philip T. Valente, H. Daniel Schantz, Cytology automation: an overview, Laboratory Medicine 32 (11) (2001) 686–690.

[30] Nanette Icho, The automation trend in cytology, Laboratory Medicine (ISSN 0007-5027) 31 (4) (2000) 218–221, https://doi.org/10.1309/NK0T-89C4-YFJD-9K5J.

[31] Monjoy Saha, Rashmi Mukherjee, Chandan Chakraborty, Computer-aided diagnosis of breast cancer using cytological images: a systematic review, Tissue and Cell (ISSN 1532-3072) 48 (5) (2016) 461–474, https://doi.org/10.1016/j.tice.2016.07.006.

[32] Wasswa William, Andrew Ware, Annabella Habinka Basaza-Ejiri, Johnes Obungoloch, A review of image analysis and machine learning techniques for automated cervical cancer screening from pap-smear images, Computer Methods and Programs in Biomedicine (ISSN 0169-2607) 164 (2018) 15–22, https://doi.org/10.1016/j.cmpb.2018.05.034, http://www.sciencedirect.com/science/article/pii/S0169260717307459.

[33] M.M. Rahaman, C. Li, X. Wu, Y. Yao, Z. Hu, T. Jiang, X. Li, S. Qi, A survey for cervical cytopathology image analysis using deep learning, IEEE Access 8 (2020) 61687–61710.

[34] Teresa Conceição, Cristiana Braga, Luís Rosado, Maria João M. Vasconcelos, A review of computational methods for cervical cells segmentation and abnormality classification, International Journal of Molecular Sciences 20 (20) (Oct 2019) 5114.

[35] Abid Sarwar, Abrar Ali Sheikh, Jatinder Manhas, Vinod Sharma, Segmentation of cervical cells for automated screening of cervical cancer: a review, Artificial Intelligence Review (ISSN 1573-7462) 53 (4) (Apr 2020) 2341–2379, https://doi.org/10.1007/s10462-019-09735-2.

[36] Khin Yadanar Win, Somsak Choomchuay, Kazuhiko Hamamoto, Manasanan Raveesunthornkiat, Comparative study on automated cell nuclei segmentation methods for cytology pleural effusion images, Journal of Healthcare Engineering (ISSN 2040-2295) 2018 (Sep 2018) 9240389.

[37] P.S. Oud, D.J. Zahniser, R. Harbers-Hendriks, M.C. van Boekel, M.C. Raaijmakers, P.G. Vooijs, The development of a cervical smear preparation procedure from the BioPEPR image analysis system, Analytical and Quantitative Cytology (ISSN 0190-0471) 3 (1) (Mar 1981) 73–79 (Print).

[38] R. Erhardt, E.R. Reinhardt, W. Schlipf, W.H. Bloss, FAZYTAN: a system for fast automated cell segmentation, cell image analysis and feature extraction based on TV-image pickup and parallel processing, Analytical and Quantitative Cytology (ISSN 0190-0471) 2 (1) (1980) 25–40.

[39] J.H. Tucker, Cerviscan: an image analysis system for experiments in automatic cervical smear prescreening, Computers and Biomedical Research (ISSN 0010-4809) 9 (2) (1976) 93–107, https://doi.org/10.1016/0010-4809(76)90033-1.

[40] I. Al, J.S. Ploem, Detection of suspicious cells and rejection of artefacts in cervical cytology using the Leyden Television Analysis System, The Journal of Histochemistry and Cytochemistry: Official Journal of the Histochemistry Society 27 (1) (Jan 1979) 629–634.

[41] WHO (World Health Organization) report, https://www.who.int/cancer/prevention/diagnosis-screening/cervical-cancer/en/, 2018.

[42] Angel Alfonso Cruz-Roa, Medical image datasets, https://sites.google.com/site/aacruzr/image-datasets, Jan 2014.

[43] Dr Jan Jantzen, Pap-smear (DTU/Herlev) databases and related studies, http://mde-lab.aegean.gr/index.php/downloads, 2005.

[44] Marina E. Plissiti, Panagiotis Dimitrakopoulos, Giorgos Sfikas, Christophoros Nikou, O. Krikoni, Antonia Charchanti Sipakmed, A new dataset for feature and image based classification of normal and pathological cervical cells in Pap smear images, in: 2018 25th IEEE International Conference on Image Processing (ICIP), IEEE, 2018, pp. 3144–3148.

[45] Elima Hussain, Lipi B. Mahanta, Himakshi Borah, Chandana Ray Das, Liquid based-cytology pap smear dataset for automated multi-class diagnosis of pre-cancerous and cervical cancer lesions, Data in Brief (2020) 105589.

[46] Hady Ahmady Phoulady, Peter R. Mouton, A new cervical cytology dataset for nucleus detection and image classification (Cervix93) and methods for cervical nucleus detection, preprint, arXiv:1811.09651, 2018.

[47] S.J. Pan, Q. Yang, A survey on transfer learning, IEEE Transactions on Knowledge and Data Engineering 22 (10) (2010) 1345–1359, https://doi.org/10.1109/TKDE.2009.191.

[48] Connor Shorten, Taghi M. Khoshgoftaar, A survey on image data augmentation for deep learning, Journal of Big Data 6 (1) (July 2019), https://doi.org/10.1186/s40537-019-0197-0.

[49] Soumyajyoti Dey, Soham Das, Swarnendu Ghosh, Shyamali Mitra, Sukanta Chakrabarty, Nibaran Das, Sync-gan: using learnable class specific priors to generate synthetic data for improving classifier performance on cytological images, 2020.

[50] J. Kittler, M. Hatef, R.P.W. Duin, J. Matas, On combining classifiers, IEEE Transactions on Pattern Analysis and Machine Intelligence 20 (3) (1998) 226–239, https://doi.org/10.1109/34.667881.

COVID-19: prediction, screening, and decision-making

5.1 Background

The novel coronavirus (nCoV) outbreak, which was identified in the late 2019s, requires special attention because of its future epidemics and possible global threats. Beside clinical procedures and treatments, since artificial intelligence (AI) promises a new paradigm for healthcare, several different AI tools that are built upon machine learning (ML) algorithms are employed for analyzing data and decision-making processes. This means that AI-driven tools help identify COVID-19 outbreaks and forecast their nature of spread across the globe.

In 2003 the novel coronavirus was identified in patients with SARS, and it is not a surprising event in 2020. Beside clinical procedures and treatments, artificial intelligence (AI) has significantly contributed. Several different AI tools are employed to analyzing data and decision-making processes. Their models are varied based on their data types [1–7] Often, machine learning requires a clean set of annotated data, so classifiers can be well trained (supervised learning). Even though we have a rich state-of-the-art literature, we failed to reach the point:

> *"To model an accurate classifier, how big the size of training samples should be?"*

Deep learning (DL), as an example, requires a large amount of data to be trained. Do we still wait for collecting fairly large amount of data? If so, then how big data is big? The primary idea behind the use of DL is not only to avoid feature engineering but also to extract distinct features (e.g., pixel-level nodule in image data) [8].

In what follows, we discuss on predictive modeling and imaging tools for COVID-19. We consider a broad view of predictions (and possible pitfalls) and medical imaging tools in accordance with the dataset size.

5.2 Predictive modeling and infectious disease outbreaks

The primary idea of the predictions is to make states and citizens aware of possible threats/consequences. However, for COVID-19 outbreak, state-of-the-art prediction models are failed

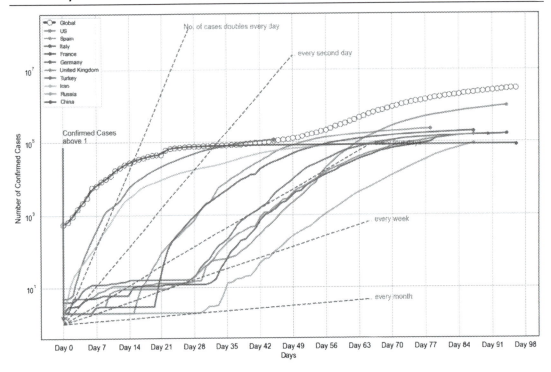

Figure 5.1: Global trend of COVID-19 confirmed cases during the first 98 days. (For interpretation of the colors in the figure(s), the reader is referred to the web version of this chapter.)

to exploit crucial and unprecedented uncertainties/factors, such as hospital settings and test rate, changes in demography, population density (including immunocompromised people), and poverty. With a high rise in deaths caused due to nCoV, immunocompromised persons (e.g., lung cancer) are at high risk. No prediction models consider immunocompromised population in terms of death cases (including recovery). Predictions can be short-term and long-term, and they rely on the aforementioned factors [4,10]. Such continuous and unprecedented factors lead us to designing complex models, rather than just relying on stochastic and/or discrete ones that are driven by randomly generated parameters. In the literature, prediction models are limited to data visualization, and they are hardly extended to simulating the data, so trends can be visualized.

To amplify/visualize COVID-19 outbreak, it requires data visualization tools. Data visualization can help estimate the trend. Figs. 5.1 and 5.2 are two examples. In Fig. 5.1, we provide an example of how we can show the COVID-19 trend for confirmed cases. Similarly, the trend of global death cases is shown in Fig. 5.2. Not to be confused, a visualization tool cannot be considered as the prediction model. Unfortunately, as mentioned earlier, in the literature, most

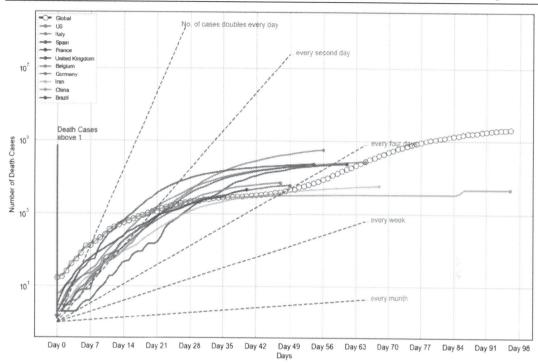

Figure 5.2: Global trend of COVID-19 death cases during the first 98 days.

of the prediction models are limited to data visualization. As an example, data simulations always help better understand the particular event(s). However, it must be limited to education/training. In simple words, simulations help us build up our intuition about how diseases work in a way that words and even static charts cannot. For visualization, distribution can be of great help (see Fig. 5.3).

Predictive analytical results hit media a lot even though tools are limited to education and training. Note that, more often, due to unprecedented nature of the situation and many uncertainties related to diseases, inaccurate information was predicted. As an example, on March 31, 2020, the White House projected 100 K to 240 K Coronavirus deaths in the next two weeks.[1] Later, on April 8, 2020, we had another media statement[2] "not every model agrees: America's most influential coronavirus model just revised its estimates downward" as previous prediction was too far from actual values (84,575 death cases in the U.S., dated May 14,

---

[1] Fox News (Andrew O'Reilly, March 31, 2020) URL: https://www.foxnews.com/politics/trump-tells-americans-to-prepare-for-a-very-painful-two-weeks-as-white-house-releases-extended-coronavirus-guidelines.

[2] The Washington Post (William Wan and Carolyn Y. Johnson, April 08, 2020) URL: https://www.washingtonpost.com/health/2020/04/06/americas-most-influential-coronavirus-model-just-revised-its-estimates-downward-not-every-model-agrees/.

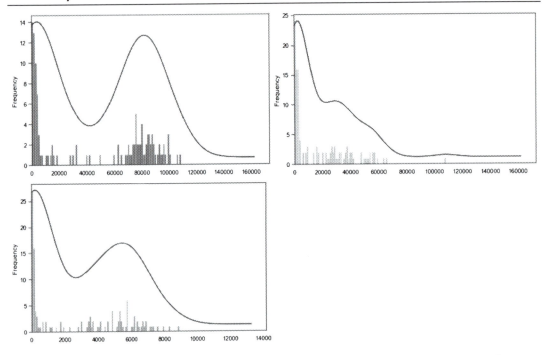

Figure 5.3: Using the first 115 days data (global): Confirmed cases (left top); Recovered cases (right top); and Death cases (left bottom).

2020). Media did not intentionally broadcast/announce inaccurate information; instead, the estimated values were based on prediction models. Not to be confused, authors are not aimed at blaming neither media nor prediction models.

Artificial and augmented intelligence (A2I) play crucial roles in understanding data by using multiple different tools/techniques. They include data analytics, machine learning, and pattern recognition, where anomaly detection is a primary element [1,9]. Predictive modeling requires exploiting comprehensive data. Missing one or two features/factors can deviate predictive values from actual ones. More often, discrete models rely on their input parameters and are application dependent. In case of continuous data (e.g., COVID-19), where there exist unavoidable uncertainties, these models behave differently. As a result, these models provide incoherent results. The primary reason behind this is lack of understanding about the particular events, that is, data sentiments and additional unavoidable uncertainties/factors, such as hospital settings/capacity, number of tests on a daily basis, demographics, and population (density) and their vulnerability in that particular region. In particular, we observed that the higher the population density, the higher the spread rate, and New York City is an example. This brings an idea that the same exact models with exact input parameters cannot be replicated to other regions. Also, immunocompromised (plus old) people need to be considered in their models; Italy is an example.

In the literature, we found three different model types for COVID-19 predictions: a) SEIR/SIR models, b) agent-based models, and c) curve-fitting models [10]. Categorically, inspired by [10], let us briefly discuss them.

1) *SEIR/SIR models:*

    Medical Research Council (MRC) Centre for Global Infectious Disease Analysis used a nonpharmaceutical intervention (NPI) model, which employed SEIR approach. In a similar fashion, Columbia University used SEIR model and forecasted number of severe cases, hospitalizations, critical care, ICU use, and deaths under different social distancing scenarios for 3-week and 6-week periods starting from April 2, 2020.[3] University of Pennsylvania used CHIME, COVID-19 Hospital Impact Model, and predicted for the next three months.[4]

2) *Agent-based models:*

    A group of research centers and universities, Fogarty International Center, Fred Hutchison Cancer Center, Northeastern University, University of Florida, and more employed the agent-based COVID-19 prediction model.[5] They forecasted based on two different scenarios: a) no mitigation and b) stay-at-home. Compared to actual data, their range can be considered even though the range is really wide.

3) *Curve-fitting models:*

    Curve-fitting model can be described by considering Fig. 5.4, where polynomial regression models are studied. As COVID-19 predictions are complex by nature, linear regression (described by the linear model $\hat{y} = w_1 x + w_o$) does not fit, and therefore no estimation is possible. In such a case, considering higher-order models would be a better fit, and that would bring an idea of higher-order polynomial regression ($\hat{y} = w_k x^k + \cdots + w_2 x^2 + w_1 x^1 + w_o$). In the figure, we address a better fit by tuning a parameter k by taking an error rate for each degree of freedom (DoF) into account. In other words, we fix the value of k when we find the best fit. In Fig. 5.4, $k = 6$ is the best fit for this data, and we conclude the regression model. Let us summarize the data:

---

[3] Mapping tool: https://cuepi.shinyapps.io/COVID-19/. Columbia University (June 23, 2020, last accessed).

[4] CHIME v1.1.5 (2020-04-08): https://penn-chime.phl.io.COVID-19 Hospital Impact Model for Epidemics (CHIME). University of Pennsylvania (April 2020).

[5] COVID-19 Model: https://covid19.gleamproject.org/#model. Northeastern University, Fogarty International Center, Fred Hutchison Cancer Center, and University of Florida (May 15, 2020, last accessed).

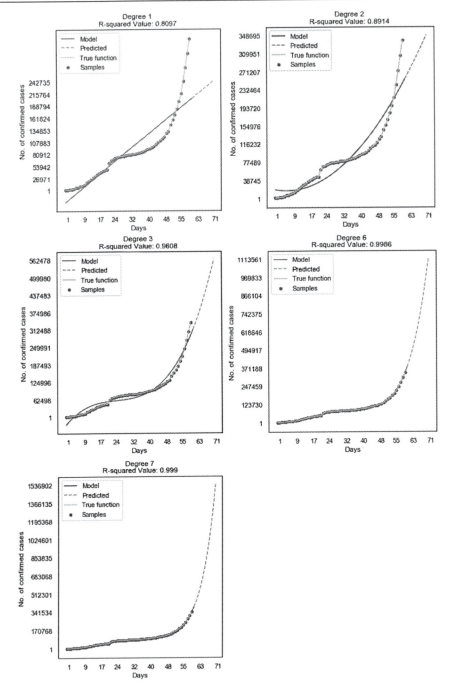

Figure 5.4: Curve fitting model using global data (the first 71 days data): polynomial regression model (predictions with different orders).

Error for each DoF (%): [32.94, 36.35, 23.08, 4.76, 4.6, 5.94, 4.27, 4.73]
DoF (selection): 6
Weights: $[4.452^{-5}, -5.31^{-3}, 3.79^{-1}, -1.91^{1}, 4.89^{2}, -1.92^{3}, 2.83^{3}]$
Model:

$$\hat{y}: 4.452^{-5}x^6 - 5.31^{-3}x^5 + 3.79^{-1}x^4 - 1.91^{1}x^3 + 4.89^{2}x^2 - 1.92^{3}x^1 + 2.83^{3}$$

On the whole, curve-fitting model is brittle. It does not predict the long-term behavior. In Fig. 5.4, we predict possible confirmed cases for the next five days.

Los Alamos National Laboratory (LANL) and the Institute for Health Metrics and Evaluation (IHME) employed a curve-fitting technique.[6,7] LANL's best guess was for California state as of April 08, 2020, 4,082 deaths (compared to 2,974 actual deaths, dated May 14, 2020). IHME's predictions varied over time.

In the literature, models are transparent enough in terms of how they were built. However, their predictions were far from actual values. Not to be confused, as input parameters vary, their models forecasted different results. Besides, no models integrate factors, such as social distancing and/or 100% lockdown. Other than aforementioned three different models, the authors used machine learning and/or deep learning models that are built on statistics and probabilities.

In machine learning, we call such models "garbage-in garbage-out",[8,9] as they predict values far from what they are. Stochastic models require fairly large amount of data to tune/stabilize their randomly generated parameters. Unlike the data-independent or discrete model, we are now required to employ mathematically proved data-driven models that have luxury to dynamically tune parameters over time.

It is a time to revisit how complex a model can be if we consider unprecedented events/factors (including social factors). As scientists, we do not like to limit to win over others in terms of validation; we rather focus on developing a prediction tool that is scalable and generalizable for any upcoming infectious disease outbreaks. Within the scope, it is a time to see whether deep neural networks[10] can be realized with thousands of parameters. Studying all data analytical tools is limited to education and training [5,6]. In case we consider using data science and

---

6   Confirmed and Forecasted Cased Data Model: https://covid-19.bsvgateway.org. Los Alamos National Laboratory (June 20, 2020, last accessed).

7   The Institute for Health Metrics and Evaluation (IHME) COVID-19 Model: https://covid19.healthdata.org/united-states-of-america (June 20, 2020, last accessed).

8   "Garbage In, Garbage Out: How Anomalies Can Wreck Your Data–Heap–Mobile and Web Analytics." heapanalytics.com (May 7, 2014).

9   Steve Goldstein. "Oops — Rick Perry says broken clock is right once a day". The New York Post (Retrieved September 19, 2019).

10   Nancy Koleva. "When and When Not to Use Deep Learning". https://www.dataiku.com (May 1, 2020).

deep learning models, their numbers of hyperparameters could potentially supersede the size of input data. In such a case, the model technically works for hyperparameters, not for input data. This is an alarming event for data science and machine learning scientists.

To sum up, the existing literature includes heavily parameterized computationally expensive tools. They neither consider unavoidable social factors nor include immunocompromised population density in that particular region. Besides, impact of immunocompromised persons (e.g., lung cancer) on mortality and/or recovery rates in COVID-19 era was not revisited [4,11]. This brings an idea of nested statistical models, where the parameters must be data-driven, and the social factors are considered as weights. The parameters are statistically adjusted based on social factors, and therefore they are dynamic in nature. Then such data-driven parameters (in terms of weights) are integrated with another statistical model for a better prediction. This, in long-term, could benefit to predict any possible infectious disease outbreaks.

5.3 Need of medical imaging tools for COVID-19 outbreak screening

Collecting large amount of data is not trivial, and we have to wait for a long time. Most of the reported AI-driven tools are limited to proof-of-concept models for coronavirus case. AI experts state that limited data may skew results away from the severity of coronavirus outbreak. The Wall Street Journal[11] reported that coronavirus reveals limits of AI health tools: some diagnostic-app makers hold off updating their tools, highlighting the shortage of data on the new coronavirus and the limitations of health services billed as AI when faced with novel, fast-spreading illnesses (Parmy Olson, February 29, 2020). In a nutshell, social medias, newspapers, and health reports, we note that conventional AI-driven tools for real-world cases (with less data) may not provide optimal performance.

Unlike other healthcare issues, for COVID-19, to detect COVID-19, AI-driven tools are expected to have AL-based cross-population train/test models that employ multitudinal and multimodal data [1]. In Fig. 5.5, we provide a better understanding of AL (in dotted red circle) with deep learning (DL) for all possible data types. In AL, expert's feedback is used in parallel with the decisions from each data type. Since DL are data dependent, separate DLs are used for different data types. The final decision is made based on multitudinal and multimodal data. For a quick understanding, two different image data are shown in Figs. 5.6 and 5.7 with clinical manifestations (for COVID-19).

---

[11] The Wall Street Journal, Coronavirus reveals limits of AI health tools (accessed February 29, 2020)), https://www.wsj.com/articles/coronavirus-reveals-limits-of-ai-health-tools-11582981201.

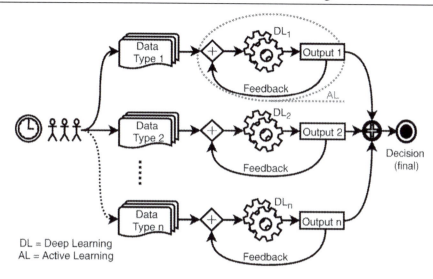

Figure 5.5: For time-series data, a schema of active learning (AL) model is provided.

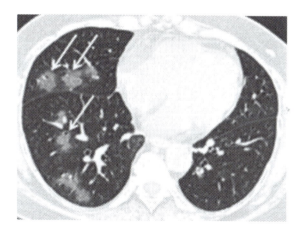

Figure 5.6: A chest CT image shows ground-glass opacities (check arrows in the right middle and lower lobes) [20].

5.4 Deep neural networks for COVID-19 screening

Following previous research papers, let us summarize deep neural networks (DNNs). As mentioned earlier, among radiological imaging data, Chest X-rays (CXRs) are of great use in observing COVID-19 manifestations. For mass screening, using CXRs, a computationally efficient AI-driven tool must detect COVID-19-positive cases from non-COVID ones (including healthy cases as well).

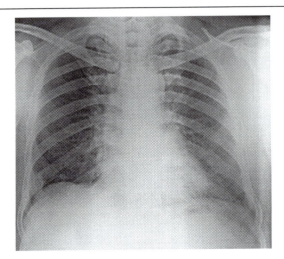

Figure 5.7: Bilateral focal consolidation, lobar consolidation, and patchy consolidation are clearly observed (check lower lung in chest X-ray).

Table 5.1:   Data collection (publicly available [12–14]).

Collection	# of positive cases	# of negative cases
C1: COVID-19	162	–
C2: Pneumonia	4280	1583
C3: TB (China)	342	340
TB (USA)	58	80

5.4.1 Truncated Inception Net: COVID-19 outbreak screening using chest X-rays [7]

Motivated by the fact that X-ray imaging systems are more prevalent and cheaper than CT scan systems, we proposed a deep learning-based CNN model, which we call Truncated Inception Net (see Fig. 5.8). Our aim is to detect COVID-19 positive cases from non-COVID and/or healthy cases using chest X-rays.

To validate our proposal, we employed six different types of datasets by taking the following CXRs into account: COVID-19 positive, pneumonia positive, tuberculosis positive, and healthy cases [12–14] (see Table 5.1). For better understanding, activation maps are shown in Fig. 5.9.

The model achieved an accuracy of 99.96% (AUC of 1.0) in classifying COVID-19 positive cases from combined pneumonia and healthy cases. Similarly, an accuracy of 99.92% (AUC of 0.99) in classifying COVID-19 positive cases from combined pneumonia, tuberculosis, and healthy CXRs was reported. We proved the viability of using the proposed Truncated Inception Net as a screening tool. For more information, we refer to [7].

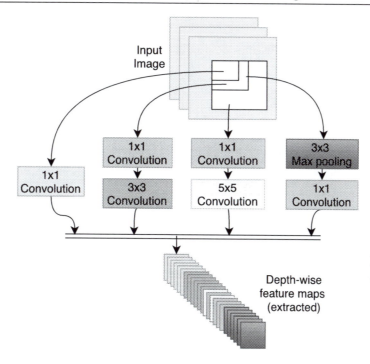

Figure 5.8: Truncated Inception network [7]. It presents the internal structure of an Inception module. Multiple-sized kernels (e.g., 3 x 3 and 5 x 5) are used to convolve with the input image, to extract features of varied spatial resolution.

Table 5.2: Generated parameters (for an image of size 25 x 25).

Layer	Parameters
Convolution	280
Dense 1	310,016
Dense 2	514
Total	310,810

5.4.2 Shallow CNN for COVID-19 outbreak screening using chest X-rays [2]

In [2], we proposed a light-weight CNN-tailored shallow architecture that can automatically detect COVID-19-positive cases using CXRs. We aimed no false negatives in our experiments. The shallow CNN-tailored architecture was designed with fewer parameters as compared to other deep learning models. For this, we refer the readers to Fig. 5.10 and Table 5.2.

The shallow CNN-tailored architecture was validated using 321 COVID-19-positive CXRs. In addition to COVID-19-positive cases, another set of non-COVID-19 5856 cases (publicly available, source: Kaggle) was taken into account, consisting of normal, viral, and bacterial

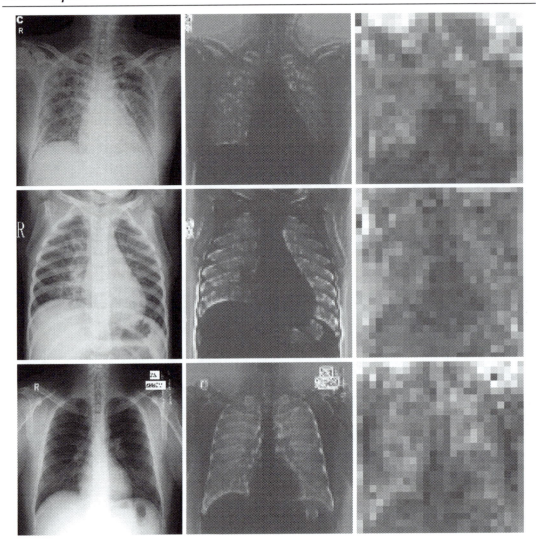

Figure 5.9: Activation maps generated by the second convolutional layer (Conv2D), the second inception module (Mixed1): COVID-19 case (top), pneumonia case (middle), and tuberculosis case (bottom).

pneumonia cases. For a better visual understanding, feature maps for COVID-19 and pneumonia cases are shown in Fig. 5.11. Using 5-fold cross-validation, we achieved the highest possible accuracy of 99.69%, sensitivity of 1.0, where AUC was 0.9995. The results were taken for a comparison with other existing deep learning models. For a comparison, the same exact set of experimental datasets was applied to other popular DL architectures, such as MobileNet [15], InceptionV3 [16], and ResNet50 [17]. The results are provided in Table 5.3.

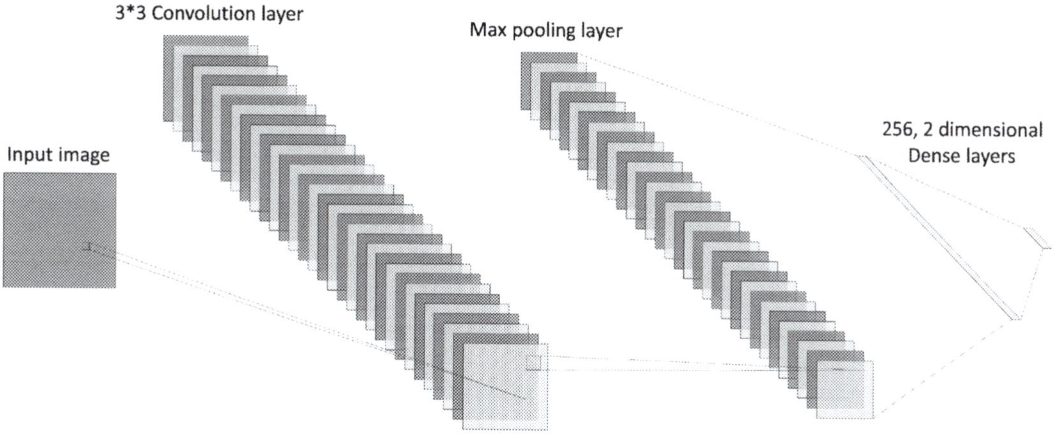

Input image

3*3 Convolution layer

Max pooling layer

256, 2 dimensional
Dense layers

Figure 5.10: A shallow CNN architecture.

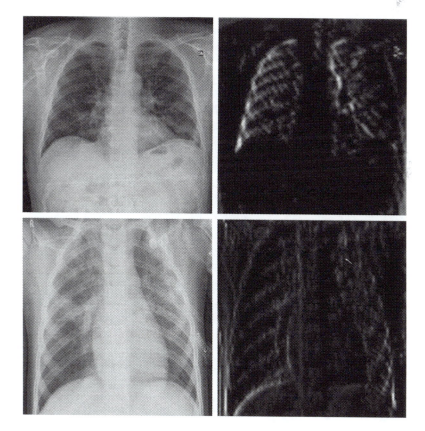

Figure 5.11: Feature maps: COVID-19 case (top), and pneumonia case (bottom).

Table 5.3: Performance comparison with other deep learning models (using balanced dataset).

Metrics	InceptionV3	MobileNet	ResNet50	Proposed CNN
Sensitivity	1.0000	1.0000	0.9252	1.0000
Specificity	0.9751	0.9938	0.9751	0.9938
Precision	0.9757	0.9938	0.9738	0.9938
False positive rate	0.0249	0.0062	0.0249	0.0062
False negative rate	0.0000	0.0000	0.0748	0.0000
Accuracy (%)	98.75	99.69	95.02	99.69
F1 score	0.9877	0.9969	0.9489	0.9969
AUC	0.9877	0.9969	0.9355	0.9995
Parameters	26,522,146	7,423,938	49,278,594	310,810

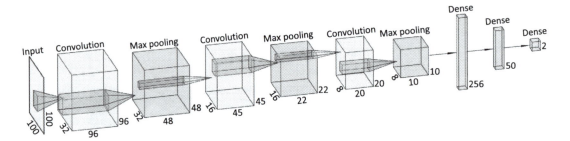

Figure 5.12: A CNN-tailored deep neural network (DNN) [3].

5.4.3 DNN to detect COVID-19: one architecture for both chest CT and X-ray images [3]

For COVID-19 screening purpose, multiple image modalities would provide higher confidence in decision-making. As chest CT and X-rays provide consistent COVID-19 manifestations [18,19], both can be considered. They can help predict, screen, and diagnose COVID-19 positive cases.

Within this scope, imaging with chest CT and X-ray images is widely used in mass triage situations. In the literature, AI-driven tools are limited to one data type, either CT scan or CXR, to detect COVID-19 positive cases. Integrating multiple data types could possibly provide more information in detecting anomaly patterns due to COVID-19. A CNN-tailored DNN that can collectively train/test both chest CT and X-rays is shown in Fig. 5.12, and its corresponding parameters are provided in Table 5.4.

Using a data collection (see Table 5.5), such a DNN architecture achieved an overall accuracy of 96.28% (AUC = 0.9808). Performance scores (using a complete dataset CXRs + CT scans) are provided in Table 5.6.

Table 5.4:   Generated parameters (different layers of the CNN architecture).

Layer	Output dimension	Parameters
Convolution 1	$96 \times 96 \times 32$	2432
Convolution 2	$45 \times 45 \times 16$	8208
Convolution 3	$20 \times 20 \times 8$	1160
Dense 1	256	205,056
Dense 2	50	12,850
Dense 3 (Output layer)	2	102
Total	–	229,808

Table 5.5:   Dataset collections.

Collections	COVID-19 cases	Non COVID-19 cases	Total
CXR [20,21]	168	168	336
CT [20,22]	168	168	336
CXR + CT	336	336	672

Table 5.6:   Performance scores (using complete dataset CXRs + CT scans).

Metrics	Scores
Sensitivity (Recall)	0.9792
Specificity	0.9464
Precision	0.9481
False positive rate	0.0536
False negative rate	0.0208
Accuracy (%)	96.28
F1 Score	0.9634
AUC	0.9808

The uniqueness behind this work is that no existing models worked on two different modalities, chest CT and X-ray images. It opens a new window for machine learning scientists that two modalities can be used in one DNN.

5.5 Discussion: how big data is big?

In what hollows, we elaborate on the use of image data for COVID-19 screening, where the focusing point is their performance in accordance with the dataset size. As mentioned earlier, we consider both image modalities, chest CT and X-ray images. For a thorough study, we refer to [23].

1) *Chest CT imaging for COVID-19 screening:*

   For COVID-19, we elaborate on the use of chest CT imaging methods based on the performance by taking dataset size into account (see Table 5.7).

   Farid et al. [24] devised a CNN-based approach to classify COVID-19 and SARS images (51 each class). Using 10-fold cross validation, they reported an accuracy of 94.11%.

Table 5.7: Chest CT imaging tools, their datasets, and performance measured in Accuracy (ACC), Area Under the Curve (AUC), Specificity (SPEC), and Sensitivity (SEN).

Authors (2020, 2021)	Dataset size	Performance (in %) ACC, AUC, SPEC, SEN
Farid et al. 2020 [24]	Dataset (Kaggle): 102 images COVID-19 +ve (51) + SARS (51)	94.11, 99.4, –, –
Hasan et al. 2020 [25]	Dataset: COVID-19 and SPIE-AAPM-NCI: 321 images COVID-19 +ve (118) + pneumonia (96) + normal (107)	99.68, –, –, –
Loey et al. 2020 [26]	Dataset: 742 images COVID-19 +ve (345) + COVID-19 -ve (397)	82.91, –, 87.62, 77.66
Li et al. 2020 [27]	Dataset: 3, 322 images COVID-19 +ve (468) + CAP (1, 551) + non-pneumonia (1, 303)	–, 0.96, 96, 90
Ardakani et al. 2020 [28]	Dataset: 1, 020 images COVID-19 +ve (510) + COVID-19 -ve (510)	99.51, 99.4, 99.02, 100
Alshazly et al. 2021 [29]	Dataset: 2, 482 images COVID-19 (1, 252) + other (1, 230)	99.4, –, 99.8, 99.6
Ni et al. 2020 [30]	Dataset: 14, 435 images COVID-19 +ve (2, 154) + pneumonia (5, 874)	82.86.54, 63, 96
Chen et al. 2020 [31]	Dataset: 30, 764 images COVID-19 +ve (13, 734) + normal (17, 030)	96, –, 94, 98

A notable study was conducted by Hasan et al. [25], who used handcrafted features from Q-deformed entropy to distinguish between lung scans, pneumonia, and COVID-19 CT slides. They achieved 99.68% accuracy on 321 subjects. Loey et al. [26] used five different DNN architectures, namely AlexNet, VGG16, VGG19, GoogleNet, and ResNet50. On dataset of 742 images, they achieved an accuracy of 82.91%, sensitivity of 77.66%, and specificity of 87.62% with ResNet50 classifier (best performance). Li et al. [27] used CT dataset of size $3,322$ subjects (468 COVI-19 cases) and achieved an AUC score of 0.96. Ardakani et al. [28] utilized $1,020$ CT COVID-19 cases and achieved the best accuracy of 99.51% (with AUC = 0.994 and sensitivity = 100%) from ResNet101 model. Alshazly et al. [29] experimented on two different CT datasets and used seven different DNNs. They used a $k (= 5)$-fold cross-validation and achieved accuracies of 99.4% and 92.9% in the two separate datasets, respectively. They also implemented a Grad-CAM to localize COVID-19 infected regions. In Table 5.7, we only show the distribution of one of the datasets, which is the largest and with the best performance. Ni et al. [30] implemented a deep learning model to train and validate with CT data acquired from 14,435 subjects. The method detects lesions, with segmentation and location with sensitivity and F1-score of 100% and 97% per-patient basis. The model also achieved a median volume of 40.10 cm^3, considering per-lung lobe basis. Chen et al. [31] developed a COVID-19 CT screening tool validated on 46,096 images and achieved the maximum accuracy of 96%.

2) *Chest X-ray imaging for COVID-19 screening:*

As before, in Table 5.8, we summarize different imaging methods and their performance in accordance with the dataset size. Let us briefly summarize them. Alqudah et al. [32] used 79 images, and the performance was 95.2% (accuracy). Horry et al. [33] used 400 images, and the achieved best performance was 83% (precision). Mukherjee et al. [2] used 260 X-ray images (130 of them were COVID-19 cases), and an accuracy of 96.92 was reported. Rahimzadeh and Attar [34] used 180 COVID-19 cases and obtained an overall accuracy of 99.5. Nour et al. [35] used a dataset of size 2,033 images (219 of them were COVID-19 cases), and their performance was 96.72% (accuracy). Brunese et al. [36] used a dataset of size 6,523 images, where 250 of them were COVID-19 cases. An accuracy of 97% was reported. Khan et al. [37] used 1251 images (COVID-19 cases = 284), and they achieved an accuracy of 89.6%. Marques et al. [38] used 1,508 images (COVID-19 cases = 504), and they achieved an accuracy of 96.70% (multiclass). Needless to mention that the aforementioned research papers (see Tables 5.7 and 5.8) have used different feature extractors, decision-making processes, and experimental setups. More importantly, for COVID-19, their dataset sizes are varied over time, and so the sources are. For a fair analysis, let us not discuss on their methodologies and/or techniqut rather focus on the dataset size. We then elaborate on the strength of machine learning and deep learning algorithms by taking the following factors into account, such as fitting, transfer learning in the era of deep learning, and data augmentation.

Table 5.8: Chest X-ray imaging tools, their datasets, and performance measured in Accuracy (ACC), Area Under the Curve (AUC), Specificity (SPEC), and Sensitivity (SEN).

Authors	Dataset size	Performance (in %) ACC, AUC, SPEC, and SEN
Alqudah et al. (2020) [32]	COVID-19 dataset: 71 images COVID-19 +ve (48) + COVID-19 -ve (23)	95.2, −, 100, 93, 3
Horry et al. (2020) [33]	COVID-19 dataset: 400 images COVID-19 +ve (100) + normal (100) + pneumonia (100)	−, −, −, 80
Mukherjee et al. (2020) [2]	COVID-19 dataset (Kaggle): 260 images COVID-19 +ve (130), COVID-19 -ve (130)	96.92, 99.22, 100, 94.20
Rahimzadeh and Attar [34]	COVID-19 dataset: 15, 085 images COVID-19 (180) + pneumonia (6, 054) + normal (8, 851)	99.50, −, 99.56, 80.53
Nour et al. (2020) [35]	COVID-19 dataset: 2, 905 images COVID-19 (219) + pneumonia (1, 345) + normal (1, 341)	98.97, 99.42, 99.75, 89.39
Brunese et al. (2020) [36]	2 COVID-19 X-ray datasets, NIH Chest X-ray: 6, 523 images COVID-19 (250) + pulmonary (2, 753) + normal (3, 520)	97, −, 98, 96
Khan et al. (2020) [37]	Dataset (Kaggle): 1, 251 images COVID-19 (284) + bac (330) + viral (327) + normal (310)	89.5, −, −, 100
Marques et al. [38]	A chest (pneumonia) and a COVID-19 dataset: 1, 508 images COVID-19 +ve (504) + pneumonia (504) + normal (500)	99.63, 97, −, 99.63

For easy understanding, we organize research papers, in both Tables 5.7 and 5.8, in accordance with the dataset size. In machine learning, we state that the bigger the data, the better the performance. This is true as we are looking at collecting all possible COVID-19 manifestations, rather than just increasing number of images. We have not observed better results from bigger datasets. If so, then how big data is big? Machine learning tools require to learn all possible manifestations related to particular diseases (COVID-19 in our case) not just the size of the dataset. However, the dataset size opens the possibility of having new cases (i.e., manifestations), which is always not the case.

Underfitting and overfitting situations are not explicitly discussed/analyzed in all these aforementioned COVID-19 screening tools (see Tables 5.7 and 5.8). They rather engaged in producing better performance scores by tuning (hyper)parameters, due to which biased results are possible.

In general, transfer learning works relatively greatly in computer vision. It may not work as expected for COVID-19 screening when we consider both image data types, chest CT and X-rays.

References

[1] KC Santosh, Ai-driven tools for coronavirus outbreak: need of active learning and cross-population train/test models on multitudinal/multimodal data, Journal of Medical Systems 44 (5) (2020) 93, https://doi.org/10.1007/s10916-020-01562-1.

[2] H. Mukherjee, A. Dhar, S.M. Obaidullah, KC Santosh, K. Roy, Shallow convolutional neural network for Covid-19 outbreak screening using chest X-rays, in: Cognitive Computation, 2021, https://doi.org/10.1007/s12559-020-09775-9.

[3] H. Mukherjee, S. Ghosh, A. Dhar, S.M. Obaidullah, KC Santosh, K. Roy, Deep neural network to detect COVID-19: one architecture for both CT scans and chest X-rays, Applied Intelligence 51 (2021) 2777–2789, https://doi.org/10.1007/s10489-020-01943-6.

[4] KC Santosh, COVID-19 prediction models and unexploited data, Journal of Medical Systems 44 (9) (2020) 170, https://doi.org/10.1007/s10916-020-01645-z.

[5] Amit Joshi, Nilanjan Dey, KC Santosh, Intelligent Systems and Methods to Combat Covid-19, Springer Briefs in Computational Intelligence, 2020.

[6] KC Santosh, Amit Joshi, Covid-19: Prediction, Decision-Making, and Its Impacts, Lecture Notes on Data Engineering and Communications Technologies, 2020.

[7] Dipayan Das, KC Santosh, Umapada Pal, Truncated inception net: Covid-19 outbreak screening using chest X-rays, Physical and Engineering Sciences in Medicine 43 (3) (2020) 915–925, https://doi.org/10.1007/s13246-020-00888-x.

[8] M. Dewey, P. Schlattmann, Deep learning and medical diagnosis, The Lancet 394 (2019) 1710–1711.

[9] Justin B. Long, Jesse M. Ehrenfeld, The role of augmented intelligence (AI) in detecting and preventing the spread of novel coronavirus, Journal of Medical Systems 44 (3) (2020) 59, https://doi.org/10.1007/s10916-020-1536-6.

[10] Josh Michaud, Jennifer Kates, Larry Levitt, Covid-19 models: can they tell us what we want to know?, in: KFF, April 16, 2020, 2020, https://www.kff.org/coronavirus-policy-watch/covid-19-models/.

[11] H.R. Bhapkar, Parikshit N. Mahalle, Nilanjan Dey, KC Santosh, Revisited COVID-19 mortality and recovery rates: are we missing recovery time period?, Journal of Medical Systems 44 (12) (2020) 202, https://doi.org/10.1007/s10916-020-01668-6.

[12] Joseph Paul Cohen, Covid-19 image data collection, https://github.com/ieee8023/covid-chestxray-dataset, 2020.

[13] Paul Mooney, Kaggle chest X-ray images (pneumonia) dataset, https://www.kaggle.com/paultimothymooney/chest-xray-pneumonia/, 2020.

[14] U.S. National, Library of medicine. Tuberculosis chest x-ray image data sets, https://ceb.nlm.nih.gov/tuberculosis-chest-x-ray-image-data-sets/, 2020.

[15] H. Chen, C. Su, An enhanced hybrid mobilenet, in: 2018 9th International Conference on Awareness Science and Technology (iCAST), 2018, pp. 308–312.

[16] C. Szegedy, V. Vanhoucke, S. Ioffe, J. Shlens, Z. Wojna, Rethinking the inception architecture for computer vision, in: 2016 IEEE Conference on Computer Vision and Pattern Recognition (CVPR), 2016, pp. 2818–2826.

[17] Takuya Akiba, Shuji Suzuki, Keisuke Fukuda, Extremely large minibatch SGD: training ResNet-50 on ImageNet in 15 minutes, CoRR, arXiv:1711.04325 [abs], 2017.

[18] Pascal Lomoro, Francesco Verde, Filippo Zerboni, Igino Simonetti, Claudia Borghi, Camilla Fachinetti, Anna Natalizi, Alberto Martegani, Covid-19 pneumonia manifestations at the admission on chest ultrasound, radiographs, and CT: single-center study and comprehensive radiologic literature review, European Journal of Radiology Open (2020) 100231.

[19] Lorenzo Ball, Veronica Vercesi, Federico Costantino, Karthikka Chandrapatham, Paolo Pelosi, Lung imaging: how to get better look inside the lung, Annals of Translational Medicine 5 (14) (2017).

[20] Covid chest XRay, online, https://github.com/ieee8023/covid-chestxray-dataset, 2020.

[21] Chest XRay (pneumonia), online, https://www.kaggle.com/paultimothymooney/chest-xray-pneumonia, 2020.

[22] COVID CT, online, https://github.com/UCSD-AI4H/COVID-CT, 2020.

[23] KC Santosh, Sourodip Ghosh, Covid-19 imaging tools: how big data is big?, Journal of Medical Systems 45 (7) (2021) 71, https://doi.org/10.1007/s10916-021-01747-2.

[24] Ahmed Abdullah Farid, Gamal Ibrahim Selim, H. Awad, A. Khater, A novel approach of ct images feature analysis and prediction to screen for corona virus disease (Covid-19), International Journal of Scientific and Engineering Research 11 (3) (2020) 1–9.

[25] Ali M. Hasan, Mohammed M. Al-Jawad, Hamid A. Jalab, Hadil Shaiba, Rabha W. Ibrahim, Ala'a R. Al-Shamasneh, Classification of Covid-19 coronavirus, pneumonia and healthy lungs in ct scans using q-deformed entropy and deep learning features, Entropy 22 (5) (2020) 517.

[26] Mohamed Loey, Gunasekaran Manogaran, Nour Eldeen, M. Khalifa, A deep transfer learning model with classical data augmentation and CGAN to detect Covid-19 from chest ct radiography digital images, Neural Computing and Applications (2020) 1–13.

[27] Lin Li, Lixin Qin, Zeguo Xu, Youbing Yin, Xin Wang, Bin Kong, Junjie Bai, Yi Lu, Zhenghan Fang, Qi Song, et al., Artificial intelligence distinguishes Covid-19 from community acquired pneumonia on chest CT, Radiology (2020).

[28] Ali Abbasian Ardakani, Alireza Rajabzadeh Kanafi, U. Rajendra Acharya, Nazanin Khadem, Afshin Mohammadi, Application of deep learning technique to manage Covid-19 in routine clinical practice using ct images: results of 10 convolutional neural networks, Computers in Biology and Medicine (2020) 103795.

[29] Hammam Alshazly, Christoph Linse, Erhardt Barth, Thomas Martinetz, Explainable Covid-19 detection using chest CT scans and deep learning, Sensors 21 (2) (2021) 455.

[30] Qianqian Ni, Zhi Yuan Sun, Li Qi, Wen Chen, Yi Yang, Li Wang, Xinyuan Zhang, Liu Yang, Yi Fang, Zijian Xing, et al., A deep learning approach to characterize 2019 coronavirus disease (Covid-19) pneumonia in chest CT images, European Radiology 30 (12) (2020) 6517–6527.

[31] Jun Chen, Lianlian Wu, Jun Zhang, Liang Zhang, Dexin Gong, Yilin Zhao, Qiuxiang Chen, Shulan Huang, Ming Yang, Xiao Yang, et al., Deep learning-based model for detecting 2019 novel coronavirus pneumonia on high-resolution computed tomography, Scientific Reports 10 (1) (2020) 1–11.

[32] Ali Mohammad Alqudah, Shoroq Qazan, Hiam Alquran, Isam Abu Qasmieh, Amin Alqudah, Covid-2019 detection using X-ray images and artificial intelligence hybrid models, Jordan Journal of Electrical Engineering 6 (2) (2020) 168–178.

[33] Michael J. Horry, Manoranjan Paul, Anwaar Ulhaq, Biswajeet Pradhan, Manash Saha, Nagesh Shukla, et al., X-ray image based Covid-19 detection using pre-trained deep learning models, engrXiv, 2020.

[34] Rahimzadeh Mohammad, Abolfazl Attar, A modified deep convolutional neural network for detecting Covid-19 and pneumonia from chest X-ray images based on the concatenation of Xception and ResNet50V2, Informatics in Medicine Unlocked (2020) 100360.

[35] Majid Nour, Zafer Cömert, Kemal Polat, A novel medical diagnosis model for Covid-19 infection detection based on deep features and Bayesian optimization, Applied Soft Computing 97 (2020) 106580.

[36] Luca Brunese, Francesco Mercaldo, Alfonso Reginelli, Antonella Santone, Explainable deep learning for pulmonary disease and coronavirus Covid-19 detection from X-rays, Computer Methods and Programs in Biomedicine 196 (2020) 105608.

[37] Asif Iqbal Khan, Junaid Latief Shah, Mohammad Mudasir Bhat, Coronet: a deep neural network for detection and diagnosis of Covid-19 from chest X-ray images, Computer Methods and Programs in Biomedicine (2020) 105581.

[38] Gonçalo Marques, Deevyankar Agarwal, Isabel de la Torre Díez, Automated medical diagnosis of Covid-19 through efficient net convolutional neural network, Applied Soft Computing 96 (2020) 106691.

Index

Printed in the United States
by Baker & Taylor Publisher Services